Who wants to be a millionaire?

HARTLEPOOL BOROUGH LIBRARIES

793.73

SPORT AND LEISURE

B❁XTREE

First published 2002 by Boxtree
an imprint of Pan Macmillan Ltd
Pan Macmillan, 20 New Wharf Road, London N1 9RR
Basingstoke and Oxford
Associated companies throughout the world
www.panmacmillan.com

ISBN 07522 15132

Produced under license from Celador International Limited
Copyright © 2002 Celador International Limited

1 3 5 7 9 8 6 4 2

A CIP catalogue record for this book is
available from the British Library.

Designed and typeset by seagulls
Printed and bound by Mackays of Chatham plc, Kent

CONTENTS

How to play

The brand new *Who Wants To Be A Millionaire? Quiz Book* designed exclusively for all Sport and Leisure buffs is finally here. Brace yourself for 1,000 new questions especially themed around Sport and Leisure topics. Whether you play on your own or compete with your friends, start with Fastest Finger First and remember to use your lifelines wisely. The *Who Wants To Be A Millionaire? Sport and Leisure* challenge awaits you.

FOR 1 PLAYER

As on *Who Wants To Be A Millionaire?*, the aim of the game is to reach £1 Million. But before you can even go on to play the game, you must first correctly answer a question from the Fastest Finger First section. You have just 30 seconds to put the letters in the correct order. When the time's up, follow the page reference at the bottom of the page to find out if you can take your place in the hotseat and begin your climb for the cash!

Once in the hotseat

Start with a question worth £100 and once you have decided on your final answer (and you're absolutely sure...) follow the page reference at the bottom of the page to find out if you're right. If your answer is correct, you can play to win £200 and start making your way up that famous Money Tree. The page where each money level begins is listed in the answer section.

As on the programme you have three Lifelines to help you on your way to £1 Million. You don't *have* to use them, but remember, each Lifeline can only be used once, so don't use them if you don't need to.

Fifty-Fifty

This option takes away two incorrect answers leaving the correct answer and the one remaining incorrect answer. The page reference at the bottom of each page will tell you where to look for the remaining answers.

Phone-A-Friend

If you have a telephone to hand (and a willing friend!) ring him/her up to help you out. You have 30 seconds (and no cheating please...) to read the question to your friend and for them to tell you what they think the answer is. If there's someone else around, ask them to time your call for you.

Ask The Audience

This works in exactly the same way as on *Who Wants To Be A Millionaire?* except we've already asked the audience so you don't have to! Simply follow the page reference at the bottom of each page to find out what our audience thought. But in the end, the decision is yours.

If you answer incorrectly at any time, you are out of the game. £1,000 and £32,000 are 'safe havens', but if you answer a question incorrectly and you have not reached £1,000 then not only are you out of the game but you will leave without a penny! If you have reached one (or both) of these havens and you answer a question incorrectly, then, depending on the stage you have reached in the game, you will leave with either £1,000 or

£32,000. If at any point during the game you are unsure of an answer and don't want to risk being out of the game, you can 'stick' at the amount you have won so far and that will be your final score. As you play, use the score sheets at the back of the book to keep a running record of the amount you have won and the Lifelines you have used.

FOR 2–5 PLAYERS

Players should take it in turns at being 'Chris Tarrant' and posing questions to the other contestants. The rules are the same as for a single player (see pages 6–7). If someone reaches £1 Million that person is the winner and the game is over. Otherwise, once everyone else is out, the person who has won the most money is the winner.

Are you ready to play? Good. With all that money at stake, we're sure we don't need to tell you to think very carefully before you give your final answer. Good luck and be sure to remember at all times the motto for *Who Wants To Be A Millionaire?* – it's only easy if you know the answer!

FASTEST
FINGER
FIRST

FASTEST FINGER FIRST

1

Starting with the earliest, put these sports in the order they were originated.

- A: Snowboarding
- B: Golf
- C: Motor racing
- D: Athletics

2

Put these courses in the order they are most likely to be seen on a French menu.

- A: Entrée
- B: Café
- C: Dessert
- D: Hors d'oeuvre

3

Starting with the oldest, place these European tourist attractions in the order they were built.

- A: Eiffel Tower
- B: St Paul's Cathedral
- C: Colosseum
- D: Louvre Pyramid

4

Starting with the most, put these traffic signs in order of the number of sides they have.

- A: Give way
- B: No entry
- C: Stop and give way
- D: One way

5

Starting with the earliest, put these boxers in the order in which they first won the World Heavyweight title.

- A: Rocky Marciano
- B: Mike Tyson
- C: Bob Fitzsimmons
- D: Sonny Liston

Answers on page 265

FASTEST FINGER FIRST

6

Starting from 'GO' on a standard British 'Monopoly' board, place these squares in the order they would be encountered.

A: Vine Street

B: Park Lane

C: Water Works

D: Old Kent Road

7

Starting with the earliest, put these players in the order in which they first won the Wimbledon Ladies' Singles title.

A: Steffi Graf

B: Venus Williams

C: Maureen Connolly

D: Billy Jean King

8

page 11

Going from right to left, place these letters in the order they appear on the middle row of a standard computer QWERTY keyboard.

A: J

B: G

C: L

D: A

9

Starting with the earliest, put these players in the order they first won the Wimbledon Men's Singles title.

A: Arthur Ashe

B: Björn Borg

C: Fred Perry

D: Pete Sampras

10

Starting with the highest, put these poker hands in order of rank.

A: One pair

B: Full house

C: Three of a kind

D: Straight flush

Answers on page 265

FASTEST FINGER FIRST

11

Starting with the earliest, put these men in the order they became manager of the England football team.

- ◆A: Bobby Robson
- ◆B: Glenn Hoddle
- ◆C: Sven-Goran Eriksson
- ◆D: Don Revie

12

Starting with the highest, put these snooker balls in order of points scored for potting them.

- ◆A: Red
- ◆B: Black
- ◆C: Green
- ◆D: Yellow

13

Starting with the closest, put these tourist attractions in order of their distance from London.

- ◆A: Taj Mahal
- ◆B: Sydney Opera House
- ◆C: Leaning Tower of Pisa
- ◆D: Eiffel Tower

14

Starting with the longest, put these sports in order of duration of normal playing time.

- ◆A: Rugby Union
- ◆B: Football
- ◆C: Basketball
- ◆D: Ice hockey

15

Put these actions in the order they would normally occur if you were taking a photograph.

- ◆A: Adjust focus
- ◆B: Load film
- ◆C: Process film
- ◆D: Print

Answers on page 265

FASTEST FINGER FIRST

16

Starting with the longest, place these athletic disciplines in order of length.

- A: Steeplechase
- B: 4 x 400 metres relay
- C: Marathon
- D: 5000 metres

17

Starting with the earliest, put these jet airliners in the order in which they first went into commercial service.

- A: Boeing 777
- B: Boeing 747
- C: De Havilland Comet
- D: Concorde

18

Put these airlines in alphabetical order.

page 13

- A: Aer Lingus
- B: Alitalia
- C: Air France
- D: Aeroflot

19

Starting with the least, put these standard golf clubs in order of the amount of loft on the clubface.

- A: Sand wedge
- B: 9 iron
- C: Driver
- D: 5 iron

20

Put these famous castles in order from north to south.

- A: Warwick Castle
- B: Windsor Castle
- C: Balmoral Castle
- D: Dover Castle

Answers on page 265

FASTEST FINGER FIRST

21

Starting with the first, arrange these words in the order they appeared in an often-used quote from the former England football manager Graham Taylor.

- A: Not
- B: Do
- C: That
- D: Like

22

Place these English football league grounds in order from north to south.

- A: Pride Park
- B: Stamford Bridge
- C: Stadium of Light
- D: Portman Road

23

Starting with the oldest, put these British landmarks in the order they were built.

- A: Tower of London
- B: Hadrian's Wall
- C: Stonehenge
- D: St Paul's Cathedral

24

Moving from a player's left corner to the right, put these pieces in order at the start of a game of chess.

- A: Queen's knight
- B: Queen
- C: Queen's rook
- D: Queen's bishop

25

Starting with the earliest, in which order would these occur in a soccer match.

- A: Extra time
- B: Penalty shoot-out
- C: Half time
- D: Playing of national anthems

Answers on page 265

FASTEST FINGER FIRST

26

Starting with the furthest distance, place these men's world records in order.

A: Discus
B: Javelin
C: Shot
D: Hammer

27

Starting with the greatest, put these sports in the order of the number of players on each side.

A: American football
B: Rugby Union
C: Basketball
D: Ice hockey

28

Starting with the shortest, place these swimming events in order of distance.

page 15

A: 400 metres freestyle
B: 100 metres butterfly
C: 4 x 200 metres medley relay
D: 200 metres individual medley

29

Starting with the farthest, put these holiday destinations in order of their distance from London.

A: Torremolinos
B: Los Angeles
C: Dublin
D: Cairo

30

Starting with the earliest, place these teams in the order of when they first played England in test cricket.

A: South Africa
B: Zimbabwe
C: West Indies
D: Australia

Answers on page 265

FASTEST FINGER FIRST

31

Starting with the easiest, place these skiing runs in order of difficulty.

- A: Blue
- B: Green
- C: Black
- D: Red

32

Put these words in the order Kenneth Wolstenholme famously said them in his commentary on the 1966 World Cup Final.

- A: Over
- B: Think
- C: All
- D: They

33

Put these words from a famous quote by Muhammad Ali in the correct order.

- A: Bee
- B: Butterfly
- C: Float
- D: Sting

34

Starting with the lowest numbered shirt, put these rugby union positions in order.

- A: Scrum half
- B: Full back
- C: Loose head prop
- D: Left wing

35

Starting with the quickest, place these British athletes in order of time taken to win their first Olympic gold medals.

- A: Sebastian Coe
- B: Sally Gunnell
- C: Linford Christie
- D: Daley Thompson

Answers on page 265

FASTEST FINGER FIRST

36

Place these words in the order they appear in a catch-phrase associated with Frank Bruno.

A: Mean   B: 'Arry

C: What   D: Know

37

Starting with the earliest, place these star signs in the order they come during the year.

A: Sagittarius   B: Libra

C: Aries   D: Leo

38

Starting with the lowest, place these sports in the order of how high the competitors get off the ground.

page
17

A: Parachuting   B: Women's high jump

C: Men's pole vault   D: 400 metres hurdles

39

Starting with the lowest, place these sportsmen in order of the number of team-mates they normally have competing with them.

A: Steve Redgrave   B: Jonny Wilkinson

C: Lennox Lewis   D: Alan Shearer

40

Starting with the greatest, put these various scores in order of the number of points normally received for each.

A: Unconverted try in rugby union   B: Goal in soccer

C: Touchdown in American football   D: Potting the black in snooker

Answers on page 265

FASTEST FINGER FIRST

41

Starting with the nearest, put these British seaside resorts in order of their distance from London.

- A: Carmarthen
- B: Dover
- C: Brighton
- D: Penzance

42

Put these parts of a triple jump in the order they should occur.

- A: Step
- B: Land
- C: Hop
- D: Jump

43

Starting at the Greenwich Meridian, put these tourist attractions in order from west to east.

- A: Sydney Harbour Bridge
- B: Pyramids of Giza
- C: Leaning Tower of Pisa
- D: Great Wall of China

44

Place these first-class cricketing counties in order from south to north.

- A: Yorkshire
- B: Somerset
- C: Nottinghamshire
- D: Warwickshire

45

Starting with the lowest, place these Britons in the order of the number of Olympic gold medals they have won.

- A: Matthew Pinsent
- B: Tessa Sanderson
- C: Steve Redgrave
- D: Sebastian Coe

Answers on page 265

FASTEST FINGER FIRST

46

Starting with the earliest, put these England cricketers in order of their dates of birth.

- A: Darren Gough
- B: David Gower
- C: Len Hutton
- D: W G Grace

47

Put these holiday destinations in alphabetical order.

- A: Chicago
- B: Cairo
- C: Cannes
- D: Canberra

48

Starting with the shortest direct distance, place these football teams in the order they would have to travel to play at Newcastle United.

- A: Leeds United
- B: Southampton
- C: Leicester City
- D: Middlesbrough

49

Starting with the smallest, put these UK game birds in order of average adult size.

- A: Snipe
- B: Pheasant
- C: Quail
- D: Woodcock

50

Starting with the earliest, put these golfers in the order in which they first won the US Masters.

- A: Tiger Woods
- B: Seve Ballesteros
- C: Arnold Palmer
- D: Nick Faldo

Answers on page 265

FASTEST FINGER FIRST

51

Starting with the first of the year, put these English public holidays in the order they occur.

A: Christmas Day

B: Good Friday

C: New Year's Day

D: Easter Monday

52

Starting with the best, put these golf scores in order of excellence.

A: Par

B: Birdie

C: Albatross

D: Eagle

53

Starting at the centre and moving outwards, put these colours on an archery target in order.

A: Red

B: Black

C: Blue

D: Gold

54

Starting with the earliest, put these tourist attractions in the order they were first opened to the public.

A: Buckingham Palace

B: Royal Festival Hall

C: Madame Tussaud's

D: The London Eye

55

Starting with the first in the year, put these tennis Grand Slam tournaments in the order they are played.

A: US Open

B: Australian Open

C: Wimbledon Championships

D: French Open

Answers on page 265

FASTEST FINGER FIRST

56

Starting with the fastest, place these sportsmen in order of the speed you would expect to see them moving in their respective sports.

- A: Stephen Hendry
- B: Michael Schumacher
- C: Frankie Dettori
- D: Michael Owen

57

Starting with the longest, place these in the order of distance the competitor would be from the target area.

- A: Alan Shearer taking a penalty
- B: Phil Taylor throwing a dart
- C: Rhona Martin releasing a stone for the house
- D: Tiger Woods teeing off on a par 4 hole

58

Put these letters in the order they might be seen on a bottle of fine, old brandy.

page 21

- A: S
- B: V
- C: P
- D: O

59

Starting with the heaviest, put these professional boxing divisions in order of weight.

- A: Featherweight
- B: Heavyweight
- C: Light welterweight
- D: Middleweight

60

Starting with the shortest, place these sporting events in order of scheduled duration.

- A: FA Cup Final
- B: US Masters
- C: Wimbledon Championships
- D: Cheltenham Festival

Answers on page 265

FASTEST FINGER FIRST

61

Starting with the youngest, put these golfers in the order in which they were born.

A: Jack Nicklaus

B: Nick Faldo

C: Gary Player

D: Tiger Woods

62

Starting with the shortest, place these sporting events in order of the distance covered.

A: Tour de France

B: Monaco Formula One Grand Prix

C: Aintree Grand National

D: Round the world yacht race

63

Starting with the shortest, put these pieces of sporting equipment in order of length.

A: Javelin

B: Relay baton

C: Pole vault pole

D: Cricket bat

64

Starting with the most, place these Winter Olympic sports in the order of how many competitors there are in each team.

A: 4-man bobsleigh

B: Ice hockey

C: Pairs figure skating

D: Skeleton bobsleigh

65

Put these sports in alphabetical order.

A: Curling

B: Canoeing

C: Croquet

D: Cricket

? Answers on page 265

FASTEST FINGER FIRST

66

Starting with the heaviest, place these sporting objects in order of weight.

A: Javelin

B: Caber

C: Table tennis ball

D: Hammer

67

Starting with the earliest, put these racehorses in the order they won the Epsom Derby.

A: Benny the Dip

B: Shergar

C: Galileo

D: Nijinsky

68

Starting with the greatest number, put these card games in order of cards dealt to each player at the beginning of a game.

A: Pontoon

B: Whist

C: Rummy

D: Poker

69

Starting with the smallest, put these sports in order according to the official size of the balls used.

A: Bowls

B: Association football

C: Table tennis

D: Snooker

70

Place these rugby league clubs in alphabetical order.

A: Wigan Warriors

B: Warrington Wolves

C: Widnes Vikings

D: Wakefield Trinity Wildcats

Answers on page 265

FASTEST FINGER FIRST

71

Starting with the fewest, put these tennis players in order of how many Wimbledon singles titles they have won.

◆A: Pete Sampras | ◆B: Jimmy Connors
◆C: Björn Borg | ◆D: Pat Cash

72

Starting with the most recent, place these athletes in order of the date of the Olympic Games they first competed in.

◆A: Jesse Owens | ◆B: Mark Spitz
◆C: Carl Lewis | ◆D: Cassius Clay

73

Starting with the highest, put these darts scores in order of value.

◆A: Outer bullseye | ◆B: Treble twenty
◆C: Double top | ◆D: Single eighteen

74

Starting with the earliest, put these drivers in the order in which they first won the Formula One World Drivers' Championship.

◆A: Damon Hill | ◆B: Juan Fangio
◆C: Nigel Mansell | ◆D: Graham Hill

75

Starting with the smallest, put these pets in order of the number of legs they have.

◆A: Rabbit | ◆B: Snake
◆C: Tarantula | ◆D: Stick insect

Answers on page 265

FASTEST FINGER FIRST

76

Starting with the earliest, put these national newspapers in the order in which they were first published.

A: The Sun
B: The Times
C: Daily Mirror
D: Daily Telegraph

77

Starting with the shortest, put these official winning horse racing distances in order.

A: Length
B: Short head
C: Neck
D: Head

78

Put these words in order to form the nickname of Stanley Matthews.

A: Dribble
B: Of
C: The
D: Wizard

page 25

79

Starting with the fewest, put these games in order of the number of balls or pieces used at the beginning of play.

A: Darts
B: Chess
C: Snooker
D: Backgammon

80

Starting with the lowest, put these karate belts in order according to the grade of proficiency of the wearer.

A: Brown
B: White
C: Black
D: Yellow

Answers on page 265

FASTEST FINGER FIRST

81

Starting with the most easterly, put these
American cities in order from coast to coast.

- A: New York
- B: Los Angeles
- C: Chicago
- D: San Francisco

82

Starting with the slowest, place these sports in order
of the maximum speed reached by the participants.

- A: Formula One
- B: Sprinting
- C: Rallying
- D: Swimming

83

Place these national rugby union
stadia in order from north to south.

- A: Twickenham
- B: Murrayfield
- C: Landsdowne Road
- D: Stade de France

84

Starting with the lowest, put these teams in order according
to the number of FA Cups won up to and including 2002.

- A: Everton
- B: Barnsley
- C: Manchester United
- D: Arsenal

85

Starting with the oldest, place these
sporting events in chronological order.

- A: 1st Modern Olympic Games
- B: 1st Aintree Grand National
- C: 1st English FA Cup Final
- D: 1st America's Cup race

Answers on page 265

FASTEST FINGER FIRST

86

Put these foods in alphabetical order.

◆A: Trifle
◆B: Treacle
◆C: Tripe
◆D: Tiramisu

87

Starting with the earliest, put these sporting films in the order they were released.

◆A: Chariots of Fire
◆B: Le Mans
◆C: Ali
◆D: Field of Dreams

88

Place these Aintree Grand National winning horses in alphabetical order.

◆A: Royal Athlete
◆B: Rhyme 'n' Reason
◆C: Red Marauder
◆D: Rough Quest

89

Starting with the furthest, put these golf clubs in the order of distance they are normally used to hit the ball.

◆A: Pitching wedge
◆B: Five iron
◆C: Putter
◆D: Driver

90

Place these 2002 Formula One Grand Prix teams in reverse alphabetical order.

◆A: Jordan
◆B: McLaren
◆C: Jaguar
◆D: Minardi

Answers on page 265

FASTEST FINGER FIRST

91

Starting with the furthest and as the crow flies, place these test match cricket grounds in order of distance from Lord's.

- A: Edgbaston
- B: Headingley
- C: Oval
- D: Old Trafford

92

Starting with the largest, put these sports in order of the size of their playing areas.

- A: Squash
- B: Netball
- C: Polo
- D: Hockey

93

Starting with the largest, put these traditional champagne bottles in order of size.

- A: Balthazar
- B: Nebuchadnezzar
- C: Magnum
- D: Jeroboam

94

Starting with the lowest, put these pre-decimal British coins in order of value.

- A: Sovereign
- B: Farthing
- C: Crown
- D: Sixpence

95

Starting closest to the floor, put these items of clothing in order according to the position you would normally wear them.

- A: Hat
- B: Socks
- C: Belt
- D: Scarf

Answers on page 265

FASTEST FINGER FIRST

96

Starting with the earliest, put these footballers
in the order in which they were born.

- A: Bobby Charlton
- B: David Beckham
- C: Nat Lofthouse
- D: Glenn Hoddle

97

Starting with the lowest, put these playing
cards in a standard pack in order of value.

- A: Queen
- B: Jack
- C: King
- D: Ten

98

Starting with the most recent, put these
Olympic venues in reverse chronological order.

- A: Barcelona
- B: Atlanta
- C: Sydney
- D: Seoul

99

Put these events in the order in which
they occur during the year.

- A: BBC Promenade Concerts
- B: Aintree Grand National
- C: Chelsea Flower Show
- D: Crufts Dog Show

100

Starting closest to the skin, put these items of
clothing in the order in which they would be worn.

- A: Gabardine
- B: Camisole
- C: Gilet
- D: Cardigan

Answers on page 265

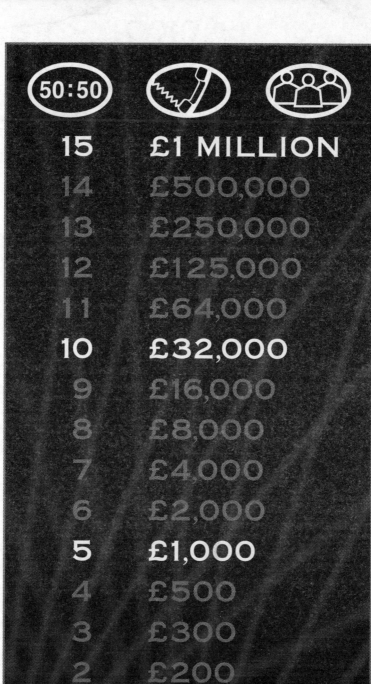

1 ◆ £100

1

By which of these methods are racehorses officially handicapped?

- A: Blindfolded
- B: Made to carry extra weight
- C: Given a head start
- D: Legs tied together

2

What do bingo players traditionally shout when they have crossed off every number on their card?

- A: Flat!
- B: Maisonette!
- C: Shed!
- D: House!

3

page
32

The dealer in a gambling game is often known as what?

- A: Fire station
- B: Hospital
- C: Bank
- D: Garage

4

Which expression is used to describe a victory for a tennis player who has won without conceding a set?

- A: Curved sets
- B: Straight sets
- C: Square sets
- D: Bent sets

5

A photographer might ask you to 'watch the ...'?

- A: Birdie
- B: Bogey
- C: Eagle
- D: Albatross

50:50 Go to page 241 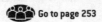 Go to page 253 Answers on page 265

1 ◆ £100

6

Which game is the climax of the NFL American football season?

- A: Nice Bowl
- B: Better Bowl
- C: Good Bowl
- D: Super Bowl

7

In which of these activities would a hook, line and sinker normally be used?

- A: Pottery
- B: Birdwatching
- C: Ballroom dancing
- D: Angling

8

Which common household pet will often purr when contented?

- A: Cat
- B: Dog
- C: Gerbil
- D: Goldfish

9

Who is one of the murder suspects in the board game 'Cluedo'?

- A: Miss Scarlett
- B: Captain Scarlet
- C: Scarlett O'Hara
- D: The Scarlet Pimpernel

10

Which of these is a popular indoor sport?

- A: Six-needle bowling
- B: Ten-pin bowling
- C: Nine-syringe bowling
- D: Four-lance bowling

50:50 Go to page 241   Go to page 253   **?** Answers on page 265

1 ♦ £100

11

In 1964 the boxer Cassius Clay changed his name to what?

- A: George Foreman
- B: Muhammad Ali
- C: Leon Spinks
- D: Sonny Liston

12

Which of these is an edging for an embroidered article?

- A: Urchin
- B: Ponytail
- C: Fringe
- D: Bob

13

In which of these sports would you normally lie down to compete?

- A: Archery
- B: Pool
- C: Darts
- D: Luge

14

Which of the following decisions might be given against you during a football match?

- A: Inside
- B: Offside
- C: Outside
- D: Overside

15

What name is given to the narrow platform along which models parade at a fashion show?

- A: Catwalk
- B: Dogstroll
- C: Rabbithop
- D: Tortoisetrot

50:50 Go to page 241   Go to page 253   ? Answers on page 265

1 ◆ £100

16

Which of these is a landmark on the
Victoria Embankment in London?

A: Pharaoh's Thimble
B: Antony's Bobbin
C: Sphinx's Reel
D: Cleopatra's Needle

17

What is done to a pack of cards
before beginning a new game?

A: Sprinkle
B: Dangle
C: Shuffle
D: Trickle

18

Which star sign is often referred to as 'The Twins'?

A: Gelati
B: Gemini
C: Jiminy
D: Germany

19

Which of these is a famous New York
sports arena and exhibition centre?

A: Madison Round Garden
B: Madison Square Garden
C: Madison Diamond Garden
D: Madison Star Garden

20

Which of these is a vehicle for transporting horses?

A: Casket
B: Box
C: Chest
D: Case

50:50 Go to page 241  Go to page 253 Answers on page 265

1 ◆ £100

21

Which of these is a type of dive?

A: Steak knife

B: Pen knife

C: Carving knife

D: Jackknife

22

What type of dancing was popularised by the BBC programme 'Come Dancing'?

A: Ballet

B: Ballroom

C: Country

D: Highland

23

Which term is used as a score in a game of tennis?

A: Love

B: Passion

C: Romance

D: Amour

24

In which decade was Carnaby Street considered to be London's trendiest shopping area?

A: Swinging sixties

B: Sinful seventies

C: Elegant eighties

D: Naughty nineties

25

Which of the following sportsmen would you normally expect to see wearing 'whites'?

A: Motor racing drivers

B: Sprinters

C: Footballers

D: Cricketers

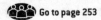 **50:50** Go to page 241   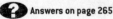 Go to page 253   **?** Answers on page 265

1 ◆ £100

26

In which Gaelic field game do players use a broad, curved stick to hit the ball?

A: Leggy
B: Footy
C: Toey
D: Shinty

27

Which decay in house woodwork can be wet or dry?

A: Tosh
B: Rot
C: Rubbish
D: Nonsense

28

Which of these games is played with balls on a table with six pockets?

A: Pool
B: Polo
C: Pelota
D: Pétanque

29

Which of these is a large seawater fish?

A: Bake
B: Make
C: Hake
D: Lake

30

Where is wine traditionally stored?

A: Cellar
B: Garage
C: Bathroom
D: Attic

50:50 Go to page 241   Go to page 253   ? Answers on page 265

1 ◆ £100

31

Which of the following would you expect to find surrounding the edge of the baize on a snooker table?

- A: Pillows
- B: Cushions
- C: Blankets
- D: Beanbags

32

Which of the following is a fast, powerful overhead shot in tennis?

- A: Crash
- B: Bang
- C: Smash
- D: Wallop

33

Which of these would an angler normally use to catch fish?

- A: Cue
- B: Baton
- C: Club
- D: Rod

34

In the garden, what name is given to a hedge or fence which lessens the force of strong winds?

- A: Windbreak
- B: Windcrack
- C: Windfracture
- D: Windrip

35

Which of these is an essential implement for making cocktails?

- A: Mover
- B: Shaker
- C: Twister
- D: Beater

50:50 Go to page 241   Go to page 253   ? Answers on page 265

1 ◆ £100

36

What is the mending of knitted garments such as socks called?

A: Blasting
B: Bothering
C: Darning
D: Blowing

37

Which of these sports does not use a ball?

A: Football
B: Tennis
C: Rugby League
D: Swimming

38

Which of these do scuba divers wear on their feet whilst swimming?

A: Flippers
B: Clogs
C: Boots
D: Sandals

39

What name is given in cricket to a very easy catch?

A: Baby
B: Bunny
C: Dolly
D: Teddy

40

Which of the following is a stroke used in swimming?

A: Butterfly
B: Moth
C: Wasp
D: Daddy-long-legs

50:50 Go to page 241   Go to page 253   ? Answers on page 265

1 ◆ £100

41

Which is the art of making designs by joining small scraps of material together?

- A: Spotwork
- B: Pitchwork
- C: Patchwork
- D: Plotwork

42

At which of the following would an archery competitor aim their arrows?

- A: Catseye
- B: Bullseye
- C: Pigseye
- D: Birdseye

43

page 40

Which of the following are used to enclose a boxing ring?

- A: Bars
- B: Chains
- C: Ropes
- D: Fences

44

Lester Piggott is famous for being which of these?

- A: Footballer
- B: Swimmer
- C: High jumper
- D: Jockey

45

Which of the following is a football league club?

- A: Crewe Mary
- B: Crewe Alexandra
- C: Crewe Elizabeth
- D: Crewe Victoria

50:50 Go to page 241 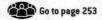 Go to page 253  Answers on page 265

1 ◆ £100

46

In which British city is Big Ben?

- A: Glasgow
- B: London
- C: Bristol
- D: Leeds

47

Which of these is a slang name for a slot machine?

- A: Back-door driver
- B: Right-wing builder
- C: Even-handed umpire
- D: One-armed bandit

48

By which of the following methods might a batsman be dismissed in cricket?

page 41

- A: Run through
- B: Run ragged
- C: Run out
- D: Run over

49

Which of these is a front row forward in rugby?

- A: Floater
- B: Liner
- C: Sinker
- D: Hooker

50

In Formula One racing, at which of the following do cars stop to be refuelled and repaired?

- A: Traps
- B: Snares
- C: Holes
- D: Pits

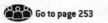 50:50 Go to page 241   Go to page 253   Answers on page 265

1 ◆ £100

51

Which receptacle is used to keep champagne cold whilst at the table?

A: Pail

B: Bucket

C: Tub

D: Pot

52

The Olympic Games feature which of these as an athletics event?

A: 10 km waddle

B: 25 km skip

C: 50 km walk

D: 100 km shove

53

Which footballing term means to run with the ball at one's feet?

A: Drip

B: Drop

C: Dribble

D: Drool

54

In rugby, what word is used for the area beyond the sidelines where the ball is considered out of play?

A: Sight

B: Smell

C: Touch

D: Taste

55

Which of these is a bruising injury often sustained by boxers?

A: Purple heart

B: Blue nose

C: Red neck

D: Black eye

50:50 Go to page 241   Go to page 253   ? Answers on page 265

1 ◆ £100

56

Which of these is the name of
a popular celebrity magazine?

A: Hello!   B: Goodbye!
C: Cheerio!   D: How Do You Do?

57

In the rules of boxing, it is illegal to hit below the ...?

A: Head   B: Shoulders
C: Chest   D: Belt

58

What colour is the ball used in a normal game of cricket?

A: Green   B: Blue
C: Black   D: Red

59

Under whose orders is the field
at the beginning of a horse race?

A: Riser   B: Beginner
C: Opener   D: Starter

60

Which of these is a Formula One Grand Prix racing team?

A: Pamela Anderson   B: Jordan
C: Melinda Messenger   D: Samantha Fox

50:50 Go to page 241   Go to page 253   ? Answers on pages 265 & 266

1 ◆ £100

61

Judo, karate, and kung fu are all described as what?

A: Plastic arts
B: Martial arts
C: Standard arts
D: Design arts

62

Which of these is the term for eggs fried on one side only?

A: Sunny-side up
B: Moony-side up
C: Starry-side up
D: Earthy-side up

63

What is the name of the circular object thrown by athletes in an Olympic event of the same name?

A: Disco
B: Frisbee
C: Ringo
D: Discus

64

Which of these is a popular sport in schools played with a 'stick' and ball?

A: Squarers
B: Triangulars
C: Oblongers
D: Rounders

65

Which of the following is a stroke played in tennis?

A: Backhand
B: Sidelong
C: Two-faced
D: Roundabout

50:50 Go to page 241   Go to page 253   ? Answers on page 266

1 ◆ £100

66

What is the match official most likely to say when Greg Rusedski is playing?

A: No hitting below the belt!

B: One hundred and eighty!

C: New balls please!

D: Foul stroke – four away!

67

Which animal represents the star sign Leo?

A: The Lion

B: The Goat

C: The Octopus

D: The Hippopotamus

68

In the world of DIY, what can be bow, panel, fret or pad?

A: Said

B: Heard

C: Saw

D: Felt

69

Which of these is an English tennis player?

A: Andre Agassi

B: Pat Rafter

C: Pete Sampras

D: Tim Henman

70

What name is given to a tree which bears cones?

A: Gaffer

B: Lucifer

C: Conifer

D: Heifer

50:50 Go to page 241　　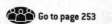 Go to page 253　　? Answers on page 266

1 ◆ £100

71

Which of these is a national daily newspaper?

A: The Daily Wireless
B: The Daily Radiogram
C: The Daily Telegraph
D: The Daily Megaphone

72

In cricket, what name is given to a run accrued when not scored by the bat?

A: Ta ta
B: Cheers
C: Bye
D: Adieu

73

Which of the following is a popular card game?

A: Blackjack
B: Bluefred
C: Brownharry
D: Bronzetom

74

Which type of free kick is awarded in a football match for certain types of infringement only, such as obstruction?

A: Vague
B: Obscure
C: Elusive
D: Indirect

75

In home decoration, what name is given to the final application of paint?

A: Overcoat
B: Topcoat
C: Lowercoat
D: Bottomcoat

50:50 Go to pages 241 & 242   Go to page 253   Answers on page 266

1 ◆ £100

76

Which of these is a prestigious British golf tournament?

A: The Shut
B: The Ajar
C: The Gaping
D: The Open

77

Which word goes before bun to give the name of a teatime treat?

A: Sink
B: Bath
C: Bowl
D: Mop

78

Which of these is an Olympic sport?

A: Synchronised jumping
B: Synchronised swimming
C: Synchronised golf
D: Synchronised hockey

79

What sort of willow is Salix babylonica?

A: Crying
B: Weeping
C: Lamenting
D: Sobbing

80

Which of these actors is a former Mr Universe and Mr Olympia?

A: Arnold Schwarzenegger
B: Danny DeVito
C: Hugh Grant
D: Robbie Coltrane

50:50 Go to page 242   Go to page 254   ? Answers on page 266

1 ◆ £100

81

Which rib bones are most commonly used for barbecuing?

A: Spare ribs

B: Extra ribs

C: Glut ribs

D: Surplus ribs

82

Which of these is a piece in a game of chess?

A: Bishop

B: Verger

C: Curate

D: Choirboy

83

In which country is the popular holiday destination, the Costa del Sol?

A: Greece

B: Kenya

C: Spain

D: Egypt

84

Which of the following might be used during a game of curling?

A: Brush

B: Dustpan

C: Mop

D: Hoover

85

To whom did Frank Bruno not lose a world heavyweight title fight?

A: Mike Tyson

B: Tim Witherspoon

C: Lennox Lewis

D: Mother Teresa

50:50 Go to page 242   Go to page 254   ? Answers on page 266

1 ◆ £100

86

Which of these is not a sign of the Zodiac?

A: Aries

B: Taurus

C: Pisces

D: Rumpus

87

What name is given to someone who collects locomotive numbers as a hobby?

A: Trainspotter

B: Railreader

C: Locowatcher

D: Choochoonoter

88

Which of the following is not a boxing weight division?

A: Flyweight

B: Middleweight

C: Cruiserweight

D: Overweight

50:50 Go to page 242   Go to page 254   ? Answers on page 266

15	**£1 MILLION**
14	£500,000
13	£250,000
12	£125,000
11	£64,000
10	**£32,000**
9	£16,000
8	£8,000
7	£4,000
6	£2,000
5	**£1,000**
4	£500
3	£300
2 ◆	**£200**
1 ◆	£100

1
What word describes plants with thick fleshy leaves?

A: Delicious   B: Sumptuous

C: Succulent   D: Scrumptious

2
Which of these is a trophy played for by amateur golf teams from Great Britain & Ireland and the USA?

A: Dry Roasted Nuts Cup   B: Walker Cup

C: Bacon Fries Cup   D: Twiglet Cup

3
In which game does one person try to guess a word one letter at a time while another person draws a gallows for each incorrect letter?

A: Executioner   B: Hangman

C: Judge   D: Court martial

4
Which of these is a newspaper often dominated by sensational stories?

A: Tabloid   B: Celluloid

C: Centroid   D: Deltoid

5
The stumps are vital pieces of equipment in which sport?

A: Basketball   B: Snooker

C: Cricket   D: Bowls

50:50 Go to page 242   Go to page 254   Answers on page 266

2 ◆ £200

6

Which of the following is a popular board game?

A: Monotony

B: Monogamy

C: Mogadon

D: Monopoly

7

What name is given to a crate of twelve bottles of wine?

A: Bag

B: Case

C: Chest

D: Tub

8

Which colour ball would you not expect to see on a snooker table?

A: Blue

B: Grey

C: Red

D: Pink

9

Which football club is not a 'United'?

A: Newcastle

B: Manchester

C: Leeds

D: Tottenham

10

What is stamped on silver and gold objects when they have passed a quality test?

A: Lobbymark

B: Kitchenmark

C: Hallmark

D: Loomark

50:50 Go to page 242   Go to page 254   Answers on page 266

2 ◆ £200

11

Which of these is a discipline in men's gymnastics?

A: Pommel pig

B: Pommel horse

C: Pommel sheep

D: Pommel goat

12

What sort of boats are most likely to be seen on British canals?

A: Thin

B: Narrow

C: Wide

D: Fat

13

Which of the following moves might be executed by a basketball player?

A: Dunk

B: Skunk

C: Mink

D: Sink

14

What name is given to the player who delivers the ball to the batter in baseball?

A: Bowler

B: Shooter

C: Server

D: Pitcher

15

Which type of paint has a hard, shiny durable finish?

A: Undercoat

B: Gloss

C: Poster

D: Emulsion

50:50 Go to page 242   Go to page 254   ? Answers on page 266

2 ◆ £200

16

The Tour de France is a famous event in which sport?

A: Horse racing

B: Cycling

C: Swimming

D: Formula One motor racing

17

Which of these would you have expected to measure over 26 miles in length?

A: Mars bar

B: Twix

C: Turkish Delight

D: Marathon

18

In which sport might you use an iron?

A: Squash

B: Golf

C: Hockey

D: Basketball

19

Which of these is a game similar to bingo?

A: Lotto

B: Putto

C: Ditto

D: Motto

20

Which three-letter abbreviation is used in cricket to describe a dismissal?

A: MCC

B: DNB

C: SOS

D: LBW

50:50 Go to page 242   Go to page 254   ? Answers on page 266

2 ◆ £200

21

What name is given to a strong West Country cider?

A: Scuffy

B: Scrummy

C: Scrumpy

D: Scrubby

22

Which form of motor racing usually takes place over 1/4 of a mile on a straight track?

A: Drag racing

B: Haul racing

C: Tug racing

D: Yank racing

23

Which of these is a type of steak?

A: Tenderleg

B: Tenderloin

C: Tenderfoot

D: Tenderhead

24

In which of the following sports is a pistol sometimes fired to signal the start of an event?

A: Croquet

B: Athletics

C: Snooker

D: Duelling

25

Which of these sports is usually performed on snow or on water?

A: Basketball

B: Gymnastics

C: Fencing

D: Skiing

50:50 Go to page 242   Go to page 254   ❓ Answers on page 266

2 ♦ £200

26

Which part of the tea plant is
normally used to make the drink?

A: Stem
B: Leaves
C: Root
D: Flowers

27

Which of these London streets is famous for its shops?

A: Cambridge Street
B: Oxford Street
C: Bristol Street
D: Leeds Street

28

What sort of sticks are used to stir cocktails?

A: Drizzle sticks
B: Swizzle sticks
C: Sozzle sticks
D: Nozzle sticks

29

Which of the following sports
is not played with an oval ball?

A: Rugby Union
B: American football
C: Australian Rules Football
D: Basketball

30

What is the horizontally extended shoot of a plant called?

A: Jumper
B: Runner
C: Hopper
D: Skipper

50:50 Go to page 242　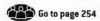 Go to page 254　? Answers on page 266

2 ◆ £200

31

Which of these is one of the five
classics of English horseracing?

A: The Coventry

B: The Norwich

C: The Gloucester

D: The Derby

32

What name is given to a tennis shot which
is impossible for the receiver to return?

A: Knockout

B: Strike

C: Winner

D: Goal

33

Which of these sports is played
on an enclosed four-walled court?

A: Lawn tennis

B: Badminton

C: Squash

D: Volleyball

34

What name is given to a network of paths and hedges
through which you have to find a way to the exit?

A: Maze

B: Folly

C: Dell

D: Abbey

35

Which of these is a famous brand of sewing machine?

A: Dancer

B: Singer

C: Actor

D: Acrobat

50:50 Go to page 242   Go to page 254   ? Answers on page 266

2 ◆ £200

36

What is the British name for the board game called 'Checkers' in the USA?

- A: Breezes
- B: Draughts
- C: Currents
- D: Squalls

37

Which is the London Orbital motorway?

- A: M1
- B: M3
- C: M4
- D: M25

38

Whisky, rum and brandy are all classed as what?

- A: Beers
- B: Wines
- C: Spirits
- D: Cordials

39

Which of these might a racehorse be likely to wear during a race?

- A: Blinkers
- B: Balaclava
- C: Snood
- D: Glasses

40

What is the name of the line marking the back of a tennis court?

- A: Byline
- B: Backline
- C: Baseline
- D: Borderline

50:50 Go to page 242   Go to page 254   **?** Answers on page 266

2 ◆ £200

41

Which of the following jumps
might a figure skater perform?

A: Axel
B: Chassis
C: Crankshaft
D: Exhaust

42

Which building In London is the home of the Queen?

A: St James's Palace
B: Buckingham Palace
C: Palace of Westminster
D: Clarence House

43

Which short curved tube allows a swimmer to
breath while just below the surface of the water?

A: Heinkel
B: Nickel
C: Yokel
D: Snorkel

44

In golf, what name is given to a shot which causes the ball to
travel to the right when played by a right-handed player?

A: Piece
B: Part
C: Share
D: Slice

45

Which of these holiday destinations is in Italy?

A: Stuttgart
B: Venice
C: Madrid
D: Paris

50:50 Go to page 242   Go to page 254   ? Answers on page 266

2 ◆ £200

46

What would be tossed at the Highland Games?

A: Sabre
B: Caber
C: Trailer
D: Labour

47

Which of the following is a recognized boxing weight?

A: Hayweight
B: Cornweight
C: Grassweight
D: Strawweight

48

In photography, what word defines the transparent strips of images that are the result of having your film processed?

A: Accusatives
B: Derivatives
C: Negatives
D: Demonstratives

49

Which of these sports includes single sculls and coxless fours events?

A: Show jumping
B: Bowls
C: Archery
D: Rowing

50

Which are you most likely to hear Darren Gough shout whilst representing his country?

A: Offside, ref!
B: Howzat!
C: The chalk came up!
D: One hundred and eighty!

50:50 Go to page 242   Go to page 254   ? Answers on page 266

2 ◆ £200

51

Into what shape are the red balls on a snooker table arranged at the start of a frame?

A: Square
B: Circle
C: Triangle
D: Pentagon

52

Which golfing term is used to indicate the standard number of strokes required to complete a hole?

A: Flush
B: Stalemate
C: Tie
D: Par

53

What is the minimum number of games a tennis player must win to take a set?

A: Four
B: Six
C: Eight
D: Ten

54

Which of these is not one of the Channel Islands?

A: Isle of Wight
B: Jersey
C: Guernsey
D: Alderney

55

In what sport might a 'technical knockout' be awarded?

A: Billiards
B: Boxing
C: Badminton
D: Bobsledding

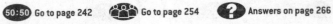50:50 Go to page 242   Go to page 254   ? Answers on page 266

2 ♦ £200

56

Which of the following sports is played on a rectangular area known as a green?

A: Squash
B: Bowls
C: Tennis
D: Baseball

57

How often are the Summer Olympic Games held?

A: Every year
B: Every three years
C: Every four years
D: Every six years

page 63

58

Which of these is a piece of metal placed in the mouth of a horse and held in position by the bridle?

A: Jot
B: Bit
C: Dot
D: Speck

59

Which famous horse race is held annually at Aintree?

A: Grand National
B: Great International
C: Gross Universal
D: Giant Global

60

What name is given to a feigned pass in rugby?

A: Puppet
B: Doll
C: Dummy
D: Manikin

50:50 Go to page 242   Go to page 254   ? Answers on page 266

2 ◆ £200

61

Which of these is a famous American stunt rider?

A: Baddy Bucknall

B: Sinful Simmons

C: Rotten Roberts

D: Evil Knievel

62

Which of these would compete at Silverstone?

A: Lennox Lewis

B: Colin Montgomerie

C: Jonah Lomu

D: Michael Schumacher

63

In baseball, what name is given to a hit that allows the batter to make a complete circuit of the bases?

A: Bullseye

B: Knockout

C: Round

D: Home run

64

Which of these is a form of motorcycle racing?

A: Accelerationway

B: Velocityway

C: Momentumway

D: Speedway

65

In which sport do skiers make their way downhill between sets of 'gates'?

A: Slowly

B: Slender

C: Slalom

D: Slipper

50:50 Go to pages 242 & 243   Go to page 254   ? Answers on page 266

2 ◆ £200

66

Which of these is not a means of
murder in the board game 'Cluedo'?

A: Poison
B: Candlestick
C: Lead pipe
D: Dagger

67

Who is a former England rugby union captain?

A: Will Carling
B: Steve Stella
C: Kenny Kronenberg
D: Harry Heineken

68

Which of these is a British snooker player and
has been a captain on 'A Question of Sport'?

A: Billy Budgie
B: John Parrott
C: Chris Canary
D: Micky Mynah

69

What name is given to the outer skin
of a lemon, often used in cookery?

A: Zone
B: Zing
C: Zenith
D: Zest

70

What score is called by a tennis umpire
when the server loses the first point of a game?

A: 15-love
B: Love-15
C: 30-love
D: Deuce

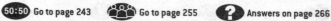 50:50 Go to page 243   Go to page 255   ? Answers on page 266

2 ◆ £200

71

Which of these is the least likely to stop a cricket match?

- A: Bad light
- B: Sunshine
- C: Rain
- D: Fog

72

Which sauce is a traditional ingredient of a 'Bloody Mary' cocktail?

- A: Tomato sauce
- B: Worcester sauce
- C: Cheese sauce
- D: Brown sauce

73

What is the area called that surrounds a hole in golf?

- A: The blue
- B: The green
- C: The red
- D: The yellow

74

Which of these is a colourful, spotted trout found commonly in lakes and streams?

- A: Sunshine
- B: Rainbow
- C: Snowfall
- D: Windblown

75

Which of these is a premier Scottish football club?

- A: Glasgow Scouts
- B: Glasgow Rangers
- C: Glasgow Guides
- D: Glasgow Brownies

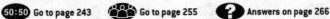

50:50 Go to page 243   Go to page 255   ? Answers on page 266

2 ◆ £200

76

Which area of London is known for its high concentration of shops, theatres, cinemas and restaurants?

- A: North End
- B: South End
- C: West End
- D: East End

77

Which of these sports held its first official World Championships in 1976?

- A: Blast ballooning
- B: Hang gliding
- C: Damn diving
- D: Perishing parachuting

78

What sort of cord opens a parachute?

- A: Tear cord
- B: Rip cord
- C: Slit cord
- D: Rent cord

79

Which of these is a version of hockey played on roller skates?

- A: Demolition derby
- B: Roller hockey
- C: Octopush
- D: Speedball

80

Which of the following is a chess piece?

- A: Duke
- B: Lord
- C: Earl
- D: King

 50:50 Go to page 243　　Go to page 255　　 ? Answers on page 266

2 ◆ £200

81

What name is given to the thread in the centre of a candle?

A: Nairn

B: Perth

C: Wick

D: Forfar

82

What name is given to a slope or course used for skiing?

A: Piste

B: Path

C: Poudre

D: Plough

83

Which of these drinks has characteristic fizzing bubbles?

A: Vodka

B: Orange juice

C: Champagne

D: Milk

84

Which of these is not an Olympic jumping event?

A: High jump

B: Long jump

C: Narrow jump

D: Triple jump

50:50 Go to page 243   Go to page 255   ? Answers on page 266

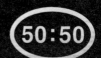  

15	**£1 MILLION**
14	£500,000
13	£250,000
12	£125,000
11	£64,000
10	**£32,000**
9	£16,000
8	£8,000
7	£4,000
6	£2,000
5	**£1,000**
4	£500
3 ◆	**£300**
2 ◆	£200
1 ◆	£100

3 ◆ £300

1

Which of these is a famous doll for boys introduced in 1966?

A: Traction Man

B: Jackson Man

C: Action Man

D: Distraction Man

2

In cricket, how many runs are scored by the batsmen during a maiden over?

A: None

B: Six

C: Twelve

D: Thirty-six

3

Which of these is a Japanese board game?

A: Stay

B: Come

C: Went

D: Go

4

In which sport was Stirling Moss a household name?

A: Archery

B: Ski-jumping

C: Motor racing

D: Football

5

Which of these is not used in decorating?

A: Undercoat

B: Limewash

C: Distemper

D: Hogwash

 50:50 Go to page 243   Go to page 255    Answers on page 266

3 ◆ £300

6

In what would you be most likely to keep tropical fish?

- A: Aquarium
- B: Apiary
- C: Aviary
- D: Arboretum

7

Which of the following might a snooker player be awarded, after an opponent has committed a foul?

- A: Free ball
- B: Cheap ball
- C: Half-price ball
- D: Expensive ball

8

What is used to fill the gaps between newly fixed tiles?

- A: Grout
- B: Grubb
- C: Gunge
- D: Glue

9

Which of these is the TV personality Jamie Oliver most likely to use?

- A: Magic wand
- B: Food blender
- C: Garden spade
- D: Paint roller

10

In horse racing, which betting term is used when the chance of winning is perceived to be equal to the chance of losing?

- A: Evens
- B: Square
- C: Quits
- D: Stalemate

50:50 Go to page 243   Go to page 255   ? Answers on page 266

3 ◆ £300

11

Which of these is a discipline in both men's and women's gymnastics?

◆A: Crypt
◆B: Dungeon
◆C: Cellar
◆D: Vault

12

Times Square is a tourist attraction in which city?

◆A: New York
◆B: Rome
◆C: Sydney
◆D: London

13

Which of these is a variety of grape used in the production of wine?

◆A: Chargrill
◆B: Charade
◆C: Chardonnay
◆D: Charcoal

14

To what did the tennis player Billie Jean Moffitt change her surname when she got married?

◆A: King
◆B: Queen
◆C: Prince
◆D: Earl

15

Which of these is not an international boxing governing body?

◆A: WBO
◆B: SAS
◆C: WBA
◆D: WBC

50:50 Go to page 243   Go to page 255   Answers on page 266

3 ◆ £300

16

In golf, what are you said to do when
preparing to take your shot?

A: Parcel the ball

B: Mail the ball

C: Address the ball

D: Send the ball

17

Which of these London areas hosts one of the
largest street carnivals in Europe?

A: Notting Mound

B: Notting Hill

C: Notting Peak

D: Notting Cliff

18

What is the full first name of the
Spanish golfer 'Seve' Ballesteros?

A: Sevastapol

B: Severiano

C: Seventeen

D: Several

19

Which of these is a cool, refreshing summer
drink containing gin, fruit and spices?

A: Mimms

B: Pimms

C: Simms

D: Timms

20

At the turn of the 19th century, where
did people go for a drink and singsong?

A: Music hall

B: Music den

C: Music parlour

D: Music cabin

50:50 Go to page 243 Go to page 255 ? Answers on page 266

3 ◆ £300

21

Which of the following is used to refer to the floor of a boxing ring?

A: Linen
B: Cotton
C: Canvas
D: Silk

22

What name is given to a small portable antique clock with a carrying handle?

A: Carriage
B: Coach
C: Car
D: Cart

23

Which of these is a fictitious trophy played for by the home countries in rugby union's Six Nations Championship?

A: Double Coronet
B: Quadruple Tiara
C: Quintuple Diadem
D: Triple Crown

24

What name is given to a small alcoholic drink?

A: Bomb
B: Shell
C: Rocket
D: Shot

25

In which sport is a point lost for a double fault?

A: Croquet
B: Cricket
C: Tennis
D: Golf

50:50 Go to page 243   Go to page 255   **?** Answers on page 266

3 ◆ £300

26

Which of the following is a form of poker?

- A: Stud
- B: Playboy
- C: Gigolo
- D: Lothario

27

What sort of 'shot' is an unskilled or random one?

- A: Jar
- B: Pot
- C: Tub
- D: Tin

28

Where in London is the Ideal Home Exhibition held each year?

- A: Duke's Court
- B: Prince's Court
- C: Earl's Court
- D: Count's Court

29

In which of the following sports are top players likely to be 'seeded' when playing a tournament?

- A: Golf
- B: Tennis
- C: Football
- D: Cricket

30

Which of the following is carried across national borders to the site of each Olympic Games?

- A: Torch
- B: Javelin
- C: Toga
- D: Laurel wreath

 50:50 Go to page 243   Go to page 255   ? Answers on page 266

3 ◆ £300

31

What nationality is Eric Cantona?

A: Spanish
B: German
C: Italian
D: French

32

Which of these is the trademark name for a hard, smooth laminate used to cover worktops and other surfaces?

A: Formica
B: Formosa
C: Fortuna
D: Formula

33

If you went into 'Bottoms Up', what would you be doing?

A: Keep fit class
B: Buying alcohol
C: Visiting a garden centre
D: Judo

34

Which of these terms describes the slices of shell often used for decorative inlay?

A: Father-of-ivory
B: Daughter-of-gem
C: Mother-of-pearl
D: Son-of-sapphire

35

In which of these sports must a player normally finish on a 'double'?

A: Snooker
B: Bowls
C: Archery
D: Darts

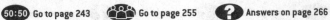 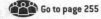

50:50 Go to page 243   Go to page 255   ? Answers on page 266

3 ◆ £300

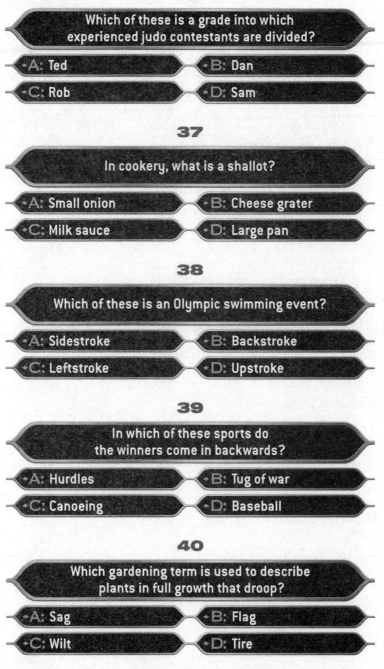

36

Which of these is a grade into which
experienced judo contestants are divided?

- A: Ted
- B: Dan
- C: Rob
- D: Sam

37

In cookery, what is a shallot?

- A: Small onion
- B: Cheese grater
- C: Milk sauce
- D: Large pan

38

Which of these is an Olympic swimming event?

- A: Sidestroke
- B: Backstroke
- C: Leftstroke
- D: Upstroke

39

In which of these sports do
the winners come in backwards?

- A: Hurdles
- B: Tug of war
- C: Canoeing
- D: Baseball

40

Which gardening term is used to describe
plants in full growth that droop?

- A: Sag
- B: Flag
- C: Wilt
- D: Tire

50:50 Go to page 243   Go to page 255   ? Answers on page 266

3 ◆ £300

41

What colour is the cue ball in snooker?

- A: Black
- B: White
- C: Red
- D: Green

42

Which boxing term refers to the delivery of two punches in quick succession?

- A: One-two
- B: One-five
- C: Five-o
- D: Ten-four

43

By what name is the penalty area on a football field commonly known?

- A: Box
- B: Safe
- C: Trunk
- D: Cell

44

Which famous department store is said to be the largest in London?

- A: Selfridges
- B: Liberty
- C: Harrods
- D: Dickens and Jones

45

In which swimming event may competitors use a stroke of their choice?

- A: Freehand
- B: Freestyle
- C: Freespirit
- D: Freeagent

50:50 Go to page 243   Go to page 255   ? Answers on page 266

46

What is the alternative name for the sausage sometimes known as 'blood pudding'?

A: White pudding

B: Red pudding

C: Black pudding

D: Blue pudding

47

Which of these appear on the Olympic flag?

A: Four triangles

B: Five coloured rings

C: Seven red stars

D: Fifty white stripes

48

Parmesan is a hard cheese from which country?

A: France

B: Italy

C: Germany

D: Switzerland

49

Which word describes the action of a horse when it jumps to the side having been frightened?

A: Shy

B: Shun

C: Fly

D: Shrink

50

In horse racing, which word means 'the state of the ground'?

A: Coming

B: Going

C: Running

D: Stopping

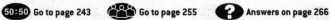
50:50 Go to page 243   Go to page 255   ? Answers on page 266

51

What sporting event has been staged in Nagano, Sarajevo, Innsbruck and Lake Placid?

A: World Athletics Championships

B: Superbowl

C: Winter Olympics

D: Soccer World Cup Finals

52

Which of these is an alternative name for moto-cross?

A: Shuffling

B: Scrambling

C: Scrabbling

D: Staggering

53

In which sport do participants stand at the oche?

A: Darts

B: Tennis

C: Baseball

D: Squash

54

Which London tourist attraction was for centuries a royal residence and the principal state prison?

A: Tower Bridge

B: Big Ben

C: Piccadilly Circus

D: Tower of London

55

What name is given to the long anchoring root of vegetables, such as carrots?

A: Sinkroot

B: Bathroot

C: Taproot

D: Plugroot

3 ◆ £300

56

Which club, founded in 1750,
is based in Newmarket, Suffolk?

A: Bowler

B: Wrestler

C: Jockey

D: Boxer

57

What name is given to the playing area in ice hockey?

A: Square

B: Rink

C: Court

D: Diamond

58

Which of these was a discipline in freestyle
skiing at the 2002 Winter Olympics?

A: Antennae

B: Receivers

C: Dishes

D: Aerials

59

Bachmann, Hornby and Peco are
famous manufacturers of what?

A: Model railway kits

B: Trainers

C: Fishing rods

D: Cricket bats

60

Which word refers to the action of throwing
a line into the water in angling?

A: Casting

B: Reeling

C: Rodding

D: Baiting

3 ◆ £300

61

In a rugby union match, the
referee is assisted by two what?

A: Sight judges
B: Touch judges
C: Flagmen
D: Parksmen

62

Which of these sports is unlikely to
have a 'pairs' or 'doubles' section?

A: Tennis
B: Rowing
C: Figure skating
D: Boxing

63

Who is a popular English snooker player?

A: Jimmy Green
B: Jimmy Brown
C: Jimmy Black
D: Jimmy White

64

Which of these traditionally works in a darkroom?

A: Poet
B: Photographer
C: Metalworker
D: Antiques dealer

65

What, inside a spirit level, confirms that a surface is level?

A: A pearl
B: A grain of sand
C: A pea
D: A bubble

50:50 Go to page 244   Go to page 256   ? Answers on page 266

3 ◆ £300

66

Which of these is a spar to which a sail is fastened to control its position relative to the wind?

A: Crash

B: Bang

C: Wallop

D: Boom

67

What do association football players wear to protect themselves from injury?

A: Helmets

B: Shinpads

C: Gloves

D: Shoulderpads

68

Which cape lies near the southern tip of Africa?

A: Good Hope

B: No Hope

C: Bad Luck

D: Hard Cheese

69

Dragging, stippling and bag graining are all techniques used in what activity?

A: Horseracing

B: Cycling

C: Bird watching

D: Decorating

70

In which sport is the UEFA Cup competed for?

A: Association football

B: Rugby Union

C: Cricket

D: Tennis

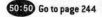 50:50 Go to page 244   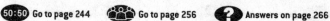 Go to page 256    ? Answers on page 266

71

What are boxers said to do to a fight if they deliberately lose the contest?

- A: Sling
- B: Throw
- C: Toss
- D: Hurl

72

What distinguished the Reliant Robin from its contemporaries?

- A: Gull-wing doors
- B: Three wheels
- C: Fuel injection
- D: First sunroof

73

Who would be expected to perform at Carnoustie?

- A: David Ginola
- B: Tiger Woods
- C: Pete Sampras
- D: Lawrence Dallaglio

74

Complete the name of the top flight Canadian ice hockey club, Toronto ...?

- A: Fig Leafs
- B: Palm Leafs
- C: Table Leafs
- D: Maple Leafs

75

What is a cricket captain said to do when he closes an innings voluntarily, before all ten wickets have fallen?

- A: Announce
- B: Declare
- C: Notify
- D: Herald

50:50 Go to page 244   Go to page 256   **?** Answers on page 266

3 ♦ £300

76

In cookery, what is the term for the process of working dough by pummelling it with the heel of the hand?

- A: Pomelling
- B: Tramping
- C: Blending
- D: Kneading

77

Who invented a puzzle cube popular in the late 1970s and early 1980s?

- A: Enrico Fermi
- B: Ernst Stavro Blofeld
- C: Erno Rubik
- D: Buckminster Fuller

78

In which of these sports may players be sent to the 'sin bin'?

page 85

- A: Football
- B: Ice hockey
- C: Tennis
- D: Croquet

79

Which board-game features squares marked 'Triple Word Score' and 'Double Letter Score'?

- A: Chess
- B: Scrabble
- C: Ludo
- D: Checkers

80

In cookery, what is a wok?

- A: A bowl-shaped pan
- B: A large spatula
- C: A double-edged knife
- D: A glass dish

 50:50 Go to page 244   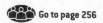 Go to page 256    Answers on page 266

50:50

15	**£1 MILLION**
14	£500,000
13	£250,000
12	£125,000
11	£64,000
10	**£32,000**
9	£16,000
8	£8,000
7	£4,000
6	£2,000
5	**£1,000**
4 ◆	**£500**
3 ◆	£300
2 ◆	£200
1 ◆	£100

4 ♦ £500

1

Which trophy is competed for at the beginning of every English football season by the previous FA Cup winners and the League Champions?

A: Charity Shield
B: Faith Cup
C: Hope Trophy
D: Grace Award

2

What name is given to the assistants who treat boxers at the end of each round?

A: Thirds
B: Seconds
C: Quarters
D: Elevenses

3

Which of these tourist attractions is in Wiltshire?

A: Stonehenge
B: Tintagel
C: Lake Windermere
D: Clifton suspension bridge

4

In a pack of playing cards, what colour are the diamonds normally?

A: Black
B: White
C: Red
D: Green

5

Which of these was a British Formula One racing driver?

A: James Hunt
B: James Fox
C: James Woods
D: James Last

50:50 Go to page 244 Go to page 256 ? Answers on page 267

4 ◆ £500

6

A potter will usually fire a pot in which of these?

A: Kino

B: Kiln

C: Kimono

D: Kettle

7

Which of these would not be much use to a competitor in the biathlon?

A: Rifle

B: Skis

C: Ski poles

D: Swimming trunks

8

What word applies to flowers or vegetables that are past full maturity and fading?

A: Plucked

B: Blown

C: Whistled

D: Strummed

9

Which of the following is traditionally known as the 'nineteenth hole' on a golf course?

A: Bunker

B: Water hazard

C: Clubhouse bar

D: Out of bounds

10

What name is given to the metal runner on an ice-skating boot?

A: Sword

B: Knife

C: Blade

D: Razor

 **50:50** Go to page 244   Go to page 256   **?** Answers on page 267

4 ◆ £500

11

Which of these is Greece's best known wine?

A: Merlot
B: Retsina
C: Rioja
D: Chianti

12

In which of these activities would a ghillie be employed?

A: Golf
B: Fishing
C: Mountaineering
D: Cycling

13

Which of these is a manoeuvre in canoeing?

A: Arctic roll
B: Eskimo roll
C: Spring roll
D: Swiss roll

14

In which field is Yves Saint Laurent a famous name?

A: Fashion design
B: Interior design
C: Car design
D: Theatrical set design

15

What are the small pieces of toasted bread, often served with soups and salads, called?

A: Crotchets
B: Cress
C: Croutons
D: Cretins

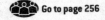 50:50 Go to page 244   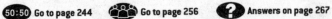 Go to page 256   ? Answers on page 267

4 ◆ £500

16

In which English city is Everton football club based?

- A: Manchester
- B: Newcastle
- C: Birmingham
- D: Liverpool

17

Where would a croupier be found?

- A: In a casino
- B: In a cutlery drawer
- C: In a golf club
- D: On a jacket

18

What is the nickname of the former cricket umpire Harold Bird?

- A: Dickie
- B: Tweety
- C: Cocky
- D: Ducky

19

Which of the following is a form of rugby union played with a reduced number of players?

- A: Threes
- B: Sevens
- C: Elevens
- D: Nines

20

What name is given to the extra thumblike toe on the front feet of dogs?

- A: Rainclaw
- B: Dewclaw
- C: Mistclaw
- D: Fogclaw

 50:50 Go to page 244   Go to page 256    ? Answers on page 267

4 ◆ £500

21

Which large Iron Age hill fort is situated south of Dorchester in Dorset?

A: Lady Castle
B: Girl Castle
C: Damsel Castle
D: Maiden Castle

22

Bratwurst is a German type of what?

A: Pork chop
B: Cabbage
C: Cracker
D: Sausage

23

What is the name of the underground railway system in Paris?

A: Le Figaro
B: Le Metro
C: Le Rodeo
D: Le Bolero

24

In curling, how is the team captain known?

A: Hop
B: Skip
C: Jump
D: Run

25

Which of these is a well-known cocktail?

A: Beijing Bowl
B: Tokyo Throw
C: Singapore Sling
D: Ho Chi Minh Chuck

50:50 Go to page 244   Go to page 256   ? Answers on page 267

4 ◆ £500

26

In card games, what name is given to a nominated card which can stand for any value?

- A: Feral
- B: Savage
- C: Free
- D: Wild

27

How does the official motto of the Olympic Games translate into English?

- A: Swifter, Higher, Stronger
- B: Who Dares Wins
- C: Going For Gold
- D: Points Make Prizes

28

What nationality is the football manager Gerard Houllier?

- A: French
- B: Swiss
- C: Belgian
- D: Italian

29

In which of these sports was Jimmy Connors a champion in the 1970s and 80s?

- A: Tennis
- B: Croquet
- C: Skiing
- D: Motor racing

30

Which of these is used in the game of badminton?

- A: Ball
- B: Puck
- C: Shuttlecock
- D: Mallet

 50:50 Go to page 244   Go to page 256 ? Answers on page 267

4 ◆ £500

31

Peter Ebdon, Ronnie O'Sullivan and Stephen Hendry are major figures in which sport?

A: Snooker
B: Squash
C: Soccer
D: Swimming

32

Which sport is played by the New York Yankees, the Boston Red Sox and the LA Dodgers?

A: Baseball
B: Soccer
C: Polo
D: Darts

33

How long is the famous Le Mans endurance race?

A: 1 hour
B: 10 hours
C: 24 hours
D: 144 hours

34

What is the nickname of ex-snooker champion Alex Higgins?

A: Whirlwind
B: Typhoon
C: Hurricane
D: Gale

35

With which of these activities are marionettes associated?

A: Pottery
B: Kiteflying
C: Dressmaking
D: Puppetry

50:50 Go to page 244　　Go to page 256　　? Answers on page 267

4 ◆ £500

36

In which sport did Olga Korbut become
a household name in the 1970s?

A: Skiing

B: Gymnastics

C: Swimming

D: Judo

37

Brook, brown and rainbow are species of which fish?

A: Trout

B: Pike

C: Tench

D: Roach

38

In rugby union, which of these is
another name for a stand-off half?

A: Fly half

B: Beetle half

C: Grub half

D: Bug half

39

Which of these would you not expect to see
wearing gloves whilst competing in their sport?

A: Lennox Lewis

B: Tim Henman

C: David Seaman

D: Mark Ramprakash

40

At which sport did Princess Anne represent
Great Britain in the Olympic Games?

A: Sailing

B: Fencing

C: Skiing

D: Equestrianism

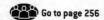 50:50 Go to page 244    Go to page 256   ? Answers on page 267

4 ◆ £500

41

Which of these is usually made with minced beef and kidney beans?

- A: Sushi
- B: Chilli con carne
- C: Won ton soup
- D: Tiramisu

42

In the game of rounders, around what does the batter run to complete a rounder?

- A: Props
- B: Pillars
- C: Posts
- D: Plinths

43

Which sport is associated with the festival known as Cowes Week?

- A: Water skiing
- B: Ice skating
- C: Yachting
- D: Canoeing

44

The Royal & Ancient is a governing body of which sport?

- A: Tennis
- B: Football
- C: Snooker
- D: Golf

45

Which of these regularly attracts the largest live attendance at any sporting event, sometimes numbering over 10 million?

- A: Tour de France
- B: Super Bowl
- C: Scottish FA Cup final
- D: World snooker championships

50:50 Go to page 244   Go to page 256   Answers on page 267

4 ◆ £500

46

What name is given to sheepdog competitions?

- A: Tests
- B: Trials
- C: Proofs
- D: Tryouts

47

How many deliveries normally make up an over in cricket?

- A: Five
- B: Six
- C: Eight
- D: Twelve

48

What is the full name of the popular music magazine, the NME?

page 97

- A: New Musical Express
- B: National Music Examiner
- C: Noise Makers' Excuse
- D: Neutral Men Escape

49

Which of these Olympic events starts in a caged circle?

- A: Javelin
- B: High jump
- C: Pole vault
- D: Hammer throw

50

How is the rugby union touring team of Great Britain and Ireland commonly known?

- A: The Tigers
- B: The Pumas
- C: The Panthers
- D: The Lions

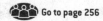 50:50 Go to page 244 Go to page 256 ? Answers on page 267

4 ◆ £500

51

In which of these sports would you attend a Basho?

- A: Boxing
- B: Stock car racing
- C: Sumo wrestling
- D: Rugby

52

Which game is played on a board which features long triangles known as 'points'?

- A: Chess
- B: Chinese checkers
- C: Backgammon
- D: Bridge

53

Which of these is not a suit in a modern deck of playing cards?

- A: Hearts
- B: Tricks
- C: Clubs
- D: Diamonds

54

In rugby, what collective name is given to the forwards?

- A: Pack
- B: Mob
- C: Drove
- D: Crush

55

Which national football team was managed by Franz Beckenbauer?

- A: Russia
- B: Czech Republic
- C: Germany
- D: Italy

50:50 Go to page 244   Go to page 256   ? Answers on page 267

4 ◆ £500

56

What name is given to a preparatory cut in glass or similar material?

A: Dozen
B: Score
C: Gross
D: Couple

57

What colour are the majority of the balls on the table at the start of a frame of snooker?

A: Brown
B: Pink
C: Blue
D: Red

58

Into which of the following is a swimming pool divided during a competition?

A: Alleys
B: Tracks
C: Lanes
D: Roads

59

In which of these sports do players not use a bat?

A: Table tennis
B: Cricket
C: Baseball
D: Croquet

60

Which cricketer captained Australia from 1984 to 1994, and established a record for the most test match and one-day international appearances?

A: Allan Hedge
B: Allan Fence
C: Allan Boundary
D: Allan Border

 50:50 Go to pages 244 & 245    Go to page 257   ? Answers on page 267

4 ◆ £500

61

Which is a form of card game?

A: Boast
B: Swagger
C: Brag
D: Crow

62

For which country did the cricketer
Dennis Lillie take 355 test wickets?

A: New Zealand
B: South Africa
C: Zimbabwe
D: Australia

63

Which of these would not have been much use to Carl Fogarty
when he was winning one of his World Championships?

A: Crash helmet
B: Leathers
C: Pitching wedge
D: Gloves

64

Which country has airports at Shannon and Cork?

A: Scotland
B: Wales
C: Ireland
D: New Zealand

65

How many holes are played in a full
round of championship golf?

A: 16
B: 18
C: 20
D: 22

50:50 Go to page 245   Go to page 257   Answers on page 267

4 ◆ £500

66

Which of these is not a top name in the world of motorbike racing?

A: Suzuki

B: Yamaha

C: Volvo

D: Honda

67

What would you normally expect to see Tony McCoy and Frankie Dettori riding?

A: Motorbike

B: Racehorse

C: Bicycle

D: 2-man bobsleigh

68

Which of the following might you find on a football field?

page 101

A: Duster

B: Sweeper

C: Brusher

D: Wiper

69

What name is given to a horse race where the prize money is of a definite amount?

A: Cruet

B: Saucer

C: Plate

D: Dish

70

Which event was introduced in synchronised form at the 2000 Sydney Olympics?

A: Diving

B: Cycling

C: Boxing

D: Fencing

50:50 Go to page 245 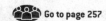 Go to page 257  Answers on page 267

4 ◆ £500

71

Which of these is a tool for spraying paint in a very even layer?

A: Fire-brush
B: Water-brush
C: Air-brush
D: Earth-brush

72

With which of these horse races is Red Rum chiefly associated?

A: The Derby
B: St Leger
C: Kentucky Derby
D: Grand National

73

Complete the name of the world famous basketball team, the Harlem ...?

A: Globetrotters
B: Earthmovers
C: Worldshifters
D: Terraformers

74

Which of the following European capital cities is known as the 'Eternal City'?

A: Rome
B: Paris
C: London
D: Berlin

75

What are the first names of the tennis playing Williams sisters?

A: Mars and Shirley
B: Pluto and Sylvia
C: Mercury and Samantha
D: Venus and Serena

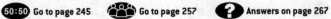

50:50 Go to page 245   Go to page 257   ? Answers on page 267

4 ◆ £500

Which charity, founded to conserve Britain's landscape and buildings, is the largest private landowner in the UK?

A: The National Faith

B: The National Trust

C: The National Hope

D: The National Belief

50:50		
15	**£1 MILLION**	
14	£500,000	
13	£250,000	
12	£125,000	
11	£64,000	
10	**£32,000**	
9	£16,000	
8	£8,000	
7	£4,000	
6	£2,000	
5 ◆	**£1,000**	
4 ◆	£500	
3 ◆	£300	
2 ◆	£200	
1 ◆	£100	

5 ◆ £1,000

1

Which of these was a founder
member of the Football Association?

- A: Accrington Norman
- B: Accrington Stanley
- C: Accrington Herbert
- D: Accrington George

2

For which country did Don Bradman play test cricket?

- A: England
- B: New Zealand
- C: South Africa
- D: Australia

3

Which sports commentator, who died in 2002, is famous
for his words '...they think its all over, it is now'?

- A: Reg Gutteridge
- B: Kenneth Wolstenholme
- C: Harry Carpenter
- D: Murray Walker

4

In the UK, the 'Give Way' road
sign is which of the following?

- A: Pentagon with blue outline
- B: Square with black outline
- C: Hexagon with green outline
- D: Triangle with red outline

5

Which of the following is not an
official principal rodeo event?

- A: Bronco riding
- B: Calf roping
- C: Bull riding
- D: Bushwhacking

50:50 Go to page 245   Go to page 257   Answers on page 267

5 ◆ £1,000

6

In which of these sports do nations compete for the Davis Cup?

- A: Tennis
- B: Cricket
- C: Golf
- D: Football

7

Which of these terms is used when a surfer falls off the board?

- A: Strike out
- B: Blow out
- C: Fall out
- D: Wipe out

8

In which continent have the modern Olympic Games never been held?

- A: Europe
- B: Asia
- C: Africa
- D: North America

9

Which of these is a nautical game played with pen and paper on a grid?

- A: Destroyers
- B: Cruisers
- C: Submarines
- D: Battleships

10

For which sport was Harry Carpenter a famous radio and TV commentator?

- A: Cricket
- B: Boxing
- C: Tennis
- D: Motor racing

50:50 Go to page 245   Go to page 257   ? Answers on page 267

5 ◆ £1,000

11

Which of these is a fielding position in cricket?

A: Glade

B: Glen

C: Gully

D: Gorge

12

What is the main ingredient of the dish sauerkraut?

A: Cauliflower

B: Cheese

C: Cabbage

D: Cucumber

13

Which football team was christened
'Busby's Babes' in the 1950s and 60s?

A: Liverpool

B: Everton

C: Arsenal

D: Manchester United

14

With which sport is the pundit John McCririck associated?

A: Football

B: Cricket

C: Horse racing

D: Motor racing

15

Which of these is a popular children's card game?

A: Snug

B: Snap

C: Snatch

D: Snag

50:50 Go to page 245   Go to page 257   Answers on page 267

5 ♦ £1,000

16

What name is given to the 10-yard area at each end of an American football field where touchdowns are scored?

A: Endzone
B: Killzone
C: Ozone
D: Boyzone

17

Which of the following sports is not played with a spherical ball?

A: Australian Rules Football
B: Basketball
C: Volleyball
D: Handball

18

How many minutes does a normal association football match last?

A: 30
B: 45
C: 80
D: 90

page 109

19

Which word is used in metalwork to mean 'altering the shape by hammering'?

A: Fashion
B: Fire
C: Kindle
D: Forge

20

What is a young plant root called?

A: Revolutionary
B: Radicle
C: Young Turk
D: Agitator

50:50 Go to page 245   Go to page 257   ? Answers on page 267

5 ◆ £1,000

21

Which New York borough was
named after the wife of Charles II?

A: Manhattan
B: Queens
C: Bronx
D: Brooklyn

22

After how many false starts are
athletes disqualified from a race?

A: One
B: Two
C: Three
D: Five

23

Which cookery writer became an entry in the
Collins English Dictionary in December 2001?

A: Jamie Oliver
B: Delia Smith
C: Nigella Lawson
D: Rick Stein

24

What is the minimum number of points a tennis player
must win to take the game when the score is deuce?

A: One
B: Four
C: Three
D: Two

25

In computer terminology, what is
denoted by .com in a domain name?

A: Community
B: Communal
C: Commercial
D: Commended

50:50 Go to page 245   Go to page 257   ? Answers on page 267

5 ◆ £1,000

26

Which of these words is normally used to describe the distinctive smells or flavours found in wine?

- A: Aroma
- B: Fragrance
- C: Perfume
- D: Scent

27

Freestyle and Graeco-Roman are styles of which sport?

- A: Skiing
- B: Swimming
- C: Wrestling
- D: Snooker

28

Which of these is a very small French biscuit or cake?

- A: Petit One
- B: Petit Two
- C: Petit Three
- D: Petit Four

29

Which of these best describes a tennis shot played just as the ball hits the ground?

- A: Lob
- B: Smash
- C: Half volley
- D: Serve

30

What do clay pigeon shooters shout when they are ready for the target to be released?

- A: Pull
- B: Lug
- C: Tow
- D: Tug

 50:50 Go to page 245 Go to page 257 ? Answers on page 267

5 ◆ £1,000

31

Which part of a sprinter's body must cross
the line first to be declared the winner?

◆A: Head
◆B: Chest
◆C: Legs
◆D: Hands

32

Originating from southern Africa,
what type of food is biltong?

◆A: Dried fruit
◆B: Dried bread
◆C: Dried meat
◆D: Dried vegetables

33

What word applies to the insulation
of hot water pipes or cylinders?

◆A: Flagging
◆B: Lagging
◆C: Clagging
◆D: Ragging

34

Which of these played football
for Coventry City and Aston Villa?

◆A: Leon London
◆B: Billy Belfast
◆C: Eddie Edinburgh
◆D: Dion Dublin

35

How is the front page of a website commonly referred to?

◆A: Pile page
◆B: Abode page
◆C: Pad page
◆D: Home page

50:50 Go to page 245   Go to page 257   ? Answers on page 267

5 ◆ £1,000

36

What name is given to the soft raised surface of cloth such as velvet?

- A: Heap
- B: Pile
- C: Stack
- D: Pack

37

Which county cricket club is based at Lord's cricket ground?

- A: Surrey
- B: Essex
- C: Kent
- D: Middlesex

38

On food packaging, what are used to denote additives and preservatives?

- A: Z numbers
- B: P numbers
- C: F numbers
- D: E numbers

39

Which of the following refers to the part of a golf course alongside the fairway where the grass is not closely mown?

- A: Coarse
- B: Rough
- C: Rocky
- D: Irregular

40

Puff, choux, and flaky are all types of which food?

- A: Omelette
- B: Apple
- C: Pastry
- D: Icing

50:50 Go to page 245   Go to page 257   ? Answers on page 267

5 ♦ £1,000

41

Which rowing term is used to describe the turning of an oar parallel to the water between each stroke?

A: Fur

B: Feather

C: Scale

D: Skin

42

Which of these is a famous fishing compendium written by Izaac Walton?

A: The Compleat Line

B: The Compleat Fish

C: The Compleat Net

D: The Compleat Angler

43

Michael Jordan and Magic Johnson are legends in which sport?

A: Ice hockey

B: Swimming

C: Basketball

D: Horse racing

44

In which of these cities is the football team Celtic based?

A: Newcastle

B: Aberdeen

C: Cardiff

D: Glasgow

45

Which of these is a type of artichoke?

A: Bethlehem

B: Nazareth

C: Jerusalem

D: Galilee

 50:50 Go to page 245   Go to page 257    ? Answers on page 267

5 ◆ £1,000

46

Which of these emblems would you expect to see on Michael Owen's shirt when he is on international duty?

- A: Thistle
- B: Three lions
- C: Shamrock
- D: Red dragon

47

Mary Quant is credited with popularising which item of clothing?

- A: Silk stocking
- B: Waistcoat
- C: Miniskirt
- D: Capri pants

48

Which of these is not an Italian cheese?

- A: Mozzarella
- B: Bel Paese
- C: Camembert
- D: Pecorino

49

With which sport is the magazine 'The Sporting Life' particularly associated?

- A: Athletics
- B: Football
- C: Horse racing
- D: Darts

50

Which of these teams took part in the 2002 Formula One Grand Prix racing season?

- A: Spears
- B: Darts
- C: Javelins
- D: Arrows

50:50 Go to page 245   Go to page 257   ? Answers on page 267

5 ◆ £1,000

51

If you went into a shop called Kookaï,
what would you be expecting to purchase?

A: Clothes
B: Cookies
C: Kitchen equipment
D: Books

52

Which team did Clive Lloyd captain to victory
in the cricket World Cup in 1975 and 1979?

A: Australia
B: New Zealand
C: South Africa
D: West Indies

53

Which of the following is the name
of a Japanese fashion label?

A: Kendo
B: Kenzo
C: Kenhom
D: Kungfu

54

What is the next word in this
football club's name, Northwich ...?

A: Anne
B: Elizabeth
C: Mary
D: Victoria

55

Which of the following is awarded for finishing
bottom of rugby's Six Nations Championship?

A: Wooden spoon
B: Rubber knife
C: Paper plate
D: Plastic fork

50:50 Go to page 245   Go to page 257   Answers on page 267

5 ◆ £1,000

56

Which of these is a major museum
on Lambeth Road in London?

- A: UK Battle Museum
- B: National Tank Museum
- C: British Fighting and Combat Museum
- D: Imperial War Museum

57

Which of these is a type of punch in boxing?

- A: Hare
- B: Mouse
- C: Rabbit
- D: Bear

58

In a game of football, how far from the ball must
defending players be when a free kick is taken?

- A: 1 yard
- B: 10 yards
- C: 18 yards
- D: 22 yards

59

How many runs are normally awarded in cricket for a shot
which crosses the boundary rope without first bouncing?

- A: 4
- B: 6
- C: 8
- D: 10

60

Which of these is a recognized breed of corgi?

- A: Cardigan
- B: Pullover
- C: Sweater
- D: Shawl

50:50 Go to pages 245 & 246   Go to page 258   ? Answers on page 267

61

By what nickname are the New Zealand test cricket team known?

- **A: Black Bats**
- **B: Black Stumps**
- **C: Black Caps**
- **D: Black Eyes**

62

Which of these is an alternative name for the game of Pétanque?

- **A: Moules**
- **B: Boules**
- **C: Joules**
- **D: Voules**

63

What name is given to the artificial spinning baits used in angling?

- **A: Lures**
- **B: Charms**
- **C: Sirens**
- **D: Temptresses**

64

Which of these is an airport just outside London?

- **A: Stamford**
- **B: Stansted**
- **C: Starworth**
- **D: Stulborough**

65

Which of these countries has never won a medal at the Commonwealth Games?

- **A: New Zealand**
- **B: Canada**
- **C: Australia**
- **D: France**

 50:50 Go to page 246   Go to page 258   ? Answers on page 267

5 ◆ £1,000

66

Which of these terms is used with reference
to a golfer whose handicap is zero?

A: Scratch

B: Tickle

C: Rub

D: Stroke

67

What gardening term means 'the pinching
out of the growing tips of plants'?

A: Halting

B: Stopping

C: Holding

D: Pausing

68

What colours are the hoops on
the first choice shirts of Celtic FC?

A: Red & blue

B: Pink & yellow

C: Black & orange

D: Green & white

69

Who, in a casino, deals cards, spins the
roulette wheel and pays out betting chips?

A: Carpenter

B: Collier

C: Chancellor

D: Croupier

70

Which of these names is most
famously associated with lamps?

A: Melanie

B: Tiffany

C: Stephanie

D: Dorothy

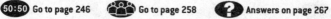

50:50 Go to page 246   Go to page 258   ? Answers on page 267

5 ◆ £1,000

71

What name is given to the area in which a showjumping competition takes place?

◆A: Court

◆B: Arena

◆C: Area

◆D: Rink

72

Which of the following would a discophile be interested in collecting?

◆A: Crockery

◆B: Gramophone records

◆C: Frisbees

◆D: Nightclubs

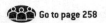 **50:50** Go to page 246   Go to page 258    **?** Answers on page 267

15	**£1 MILLION**
14	£500,000
13	£250,000
12	£125,000
11	£64,000
10	**£32,000**
9	£16,000
8	£8,000
7	£4,000
6 ◆	**£2,000**
5 ◆	£1,000
4 ◆	£500
3 ◆	£300
2 ◆	£200
1 ◆	£100

6 ◆ £2,000

1

In betting slang, how is a wager of £500 described?

A: Pony

B: Monkey

C: Donkey

D: Gorilla

2

Complete the name of this women's football team, the Doncaster ...?

A: Cats

B: Lionesses

C: Daredevils

D: Belles

3

Sugar Loaf mountain towers above which exotic holiday destination?

A: Hong Kong

B: Sydney

C: Rio de Janeiro

D: Singapore

4

What are the alternating colours on a standard roulette wheel?

A: Black and blue

B: Black and white

C: Black and yellow

D: Black and red

5

With which sport is the former broadcaster Bill McLaren chiefly associated?

A: Cricket

B: Tennis

C: Motor racing

D: Rugby Union

50:50 Go to page 246 Go to page 258 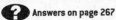 Answers on page 267

6

In horse racing, which of the following means a bet placed on a horse either to win or to be placed highly?

◆A: One way
◆B: Each way
◆C: Two way
◆D: Evens

7

In which US state is Elvis Presley's mansion, Graceland?

◆A: Alabama
◆B: Kentucky
◆C: Tennessee
◆D: Georgia

8

What is the nickname of the former world heavyweight boxing champion Joe Frazier?

◆A: Smokin' Joe
◆B: Burnin' Joe
◆C: Puffin' Joe
◆D: Coughin' Joe

9

Which of these is a popular holiday resort in Massachusetts?

◆A: Hannah's Orchard
◆B: Sissy's Paddy-field
◆C: Martha's Vineyard
◆D: Beth's Cornfield

10

What is famously cut into the chalk at Uffington in Oxfordshire?

◆A: White knight
◆B: White giant
◆C: White unicorn
◆D: White horse

 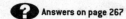

6 ◆ £2,000

11

Which of these is the action of adjusting the sails of a yacht so as to fill or empty them of wind?

- A: Cutting
- B: Shearing
- C: Trimming
- D: Shaving

12

Complete the name of the tennis star of the 1920s and 30s, Helen Wills ...?

- A: Moody
- B: Sad
- C: Sullen
- D: Sulky

13

If you are following instructions which read K2tog - what are you doing?

- A: Flying a kite
- B: Knitting
- C: Cooking
- D: Printing

14

Which word means wine which has become contaminated?

- A: Corked
- B: Oaked
- C: Barrelled
- D: Casked

15

The scissors, straddle and eastern cut-off were all styles used in which athletics event?

- A: Long jump
- B: Triple jump
- C: High jump
- D: Shot put

50:50 Go to page 246   Go to page 258   ? Answers on page 267

6 ◆ £2,000

16

Which of these is a premier Dutch football club?

- A: Ajax
- B: Vim
- C: Persil
- D: Domestos

17

In computing, what name is given to a quantity of digital information stored on a disk?

- A: Code
- B: File
- C: Digest
- D: Parcel

18

How is horse racing sometimes described?

- A: Play of princes
- B: Sport of kings
- C: Fancy of queens
- D: Fun of knaves

19

With which sport is the legendary Sam Snead chiefly associated?

- A: Baseball
- B: Tennis
- C: Ice hockey
- D: Golf

20

Plantains are a cooking variety of which fruit?

- A: Banana
- B: Pear
- C: Apple
- D: Apricot

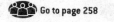 50:50 Go to page 246   Go to page 258    ? Answers on page 267

6 ◆ £2,000

21

What sort of nuts are 'marrons' on a French menu?

- A: Chestnuts
- B: Almonds
- C: Walnuts
- D: Peanuts

22

In which sport was Rory Underwood a much-capped England player?

- A: Association football
- B: Cricket
- C: Tennis
- D: Rugby Union

23

What colour is the horizontal bar on a 'No Entry' traffic sign?

- A: Black
- B: Red
- C: White
- D: Blue

24

How many lanes are there on a standard athletics track?

- A: Six
- B: Eight
- C: Ten
- D: Twelve

25

Which football club plays its home matches at Stamford Bridge?

- A: West Ham United
- B: Charlton Athletic
- C: Chelsea
- D: Arsenal

50:50 Go to page 246   Go to page 258   ? Answers on page 267

6 ◆ £2,000

26

Tapas are traditional appetisers from which country?

- A: Canada
- B: Spain
- C: Belgium
- D: Sweden

27

Which of these is a two-way radio link which became popular in the UK during the 1970s?

- A: TC
- B: AD
- C: VA
- D: CB

28

In which sport did Duncan Goodhew and Adrian Moorhouse win Olympic gold medals for Great Britain in the 1980s?

- A: Judo
- B: Rowing
- C: Cycling
- D: Swimming

29

Which is the only golf major to be held on the same course - Augusta National - every year?

- A: US PGA
- B: The Open
- C: The US Masters
- D: The US Open

30

In which sport was Britain's Barry Sheene a world champion in 1976 and 1977?

- A: Motorcycling
- B: Squash
- C: Boxing
- D: Skiing

50:50 Go to page 246 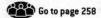 Go to page 258 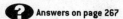 **?** Answers on page 267

6 ♦ £2,000

31

Which is a common abbreviation for a computer screen?

- A: VHS
- B: VCR
- C: VDU
- D: VTR

32

For which sport is Churchill Downs a famous venue in the USA?

- A: Horse racing
- B: Tennis
- C: Baseball
- D: American football

33

Which three letters go before 'Eindhoven' to make the name of a leading Dutch football club?

- A: KLM
- B: VIM
- C: DIK
- D: PSV

34

What sort of board forms the facing at the gable end of a roof?

- A: Barge
- B: Smack
- C: Ketch
- D: Clipper

35

Which former British athlete was the founder of the London Marathon?

- A: Chris Brasher
- B: David Hemery
- C: Lynn Davies
- D: Daley Thompson

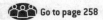 50:50 Go to page 246   Go to page 258   ? Answers on page 267

6 ◆ £2,000

36

In Indian cooking, chapati and naan are both types of what?

- A: Meat
- B: Bread
- C: Rice
- D: Sauce

37

Which of these is not a UK motor racing circuit?

- A: Silverstone
- B: Brands Hatch
- C: Ascot
- D: Oulton Park

38

In which of these sports are competitors awarded the Golden Gloves?

- A: Baseball
- B: Cricket
- C: Motor racing
- D: Boxing

39

What does the 'T' in the boxing term 'TKO' stand for?

- A: Technical
- B: Temporary
- C: Title
- D: Total

40

In which of these sports are forward passes and 'knock ons' penalised?

- A: Cricket
- B: Soccer
- C: Baseball
- D: Rugby Union

50:50 Go to page 246   Go to page 258   Answers on page 267

6 ◆ £2,000

41

Which of these is sometimes known as
'English white' or 'white on white' embroidery?

- A: Broderie Anglaise
- B: Broderie Française
- C: Broderie Espagnole
- D: Broderie Suede

42

With which sport are the Irish venues of
Punchestown and the Curragh chiefly associated?

- A: Motor racing
- B: Athletics
- C: Sailing
- D: Horse racing

43

The grounds of which famous country house
were partly converted into a safari park in 1966?

- A: Blenheim Palace
- B: Audley End
- C: Chatsworth
- D: Longleat

44

The autobiography of which famous former footballer
is entitled 'The Good, the Bad and the Bubbly'?

- A: Stanley Matthews
- B: George Best
- C: Bobby Charlton
- D: Jack Charlton

45

In which sport do opponents
compete for the Lonsdale Belt?

- A: Boxing
- B: Fencing
- C: Judo
- D: Wrestling

50:50 Go to page 246 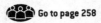 Go to page 258 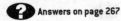 Answers on page 267

6 ◆ £2,000

46

For how many days is a cricket test match normally scheduled?

A: One
B: Three
C: Five
D: Seven

47

What was the nationality of the legendary athlete Jesse Owens?

A: Canadian
B: British
C: Australian
D: American

48

Which London football club's home ground is known as Highbury?

A: Chelsea
B: Millwall
C: Charlton Athletic
D: Arsenal

49

What would an angler normally put in a keepnet?

A: Rod
B: Bait
C: Tackle
D: Fish

50

In American football, when a quarterback is tackled he is said to be what?

A: Fired
B: Sacked
C: Dismissed
D: Axed

50:50 Go to page 246   Go to page 258   ? Answers on page 267

51

Which of these is one of the Balearic Islands?

A: Corsica
B: Como
C: Ibiza
D: Skyros

52

With which of these scores can a darts player achieve to finish a game with only one dart?

A: 180
B: 50
C: 25
D: 60

53

What is used in woodwork to hold something steady while it is being worked upon?

A: Vice
B: Plane
C: Bore
D: Rasp

54

Discounting penalty strokes, what is the official maximum break possible in snooker?

A: 25
B: 101
C: 147
D: 501

55

McLaren, Arrows, and Williams are teams in which sport?

A: Formula One
B: Swimming
C: Lacrosse
D: Show jumping

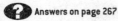

50:50 Go to page 246   Go to page 258   **?** Answers on page 267

6 ◆ £2,000

56

With which game is Anatoly Karpov chiefly associated?

- A: Bridge
- B: Backgammon
- C: Chess
- D: Darts

57

Which of these is a Hindu discipline used by many as a form of exercise and relaxation?

- A: Tae kwon do
- B: Reiki
- C: Yoga
- D: Feng shui

58

In which year did Roger Bannister break the 'four-minute mile'?

- A: 1904
- B: 1934
- C: 1954
- D: 1974

59

Of which city is Piraeus the main port?

- A: Rome
- B: Amsterdam
- C: Marseilles
- D: Athens

60

Averaging only 13 centimetres in height and 2 kilograms in weight, which is the smallest recognized breed of domestic dog?

- A: Basset hound
- B: Dachshund
- C: Fox terrier
- D: Chihuahua

50:50 Go to page 246   Go to page 258   ? Answers on page 267

6 ◆ £2,000

61

What is the standard length in metres
of an Olympic-sized swimming pool?

A: 25

B: 50

C: 75

D: 100

62

Which of these is a French football league team?

A: Focus

B: Aperture

C: Filter

D: Lens

63

At the beginning of a normal game of 'Scrabble',
how many tiles does each player take from the pool?

A: One

B: Seven

C: Twelve

D: Thirty

64

Which of these is a former British javelin champion?

A: Tessa Wyatt

B: Tessa Jowell

C: Tessa Sanderson

D: Tessa Smith

65

In which sport did Willie John McBride
represent Ireland 63 times?

A: Association Football

B: Show jumping

C: Hockey

D: Rugby Union

50:50 Go to page 247   Go to page 258   ? Answers on page 267

6 ◆ £2,000

66

Origami is the Japanese art of what?

A: Flower-arranging

B: Thread-knotting

C: Wood-carving

D: Paper-folding

67

In which target ball game are the balls likely to be 'spots' and 'stripes'?

A: Snooker

B: Skittles

C: Boules

D: Pool

68

Which of these is a famous fashion designer?

page
135

A: Giorgio Moroder

B: Giorgio Belladonna

C: Giorgio Morandi

D: Giorgio Armani

50:50 Go to page 247   Go to page 259   ? Answers on page 267

50:50

15	**£1 MILLION**
14	£500,000
13	£250,000
12	£125,000
11	£64,000
10	**£32,000**
9	£16,000
8	£8,000
7 ◆	**£4,000**
6 ◆	£2,000
5 ◆	£1,000
4 ◆	£500
3 ◆	£300
2 ◆	£200
1 ◆	£100

7 ◆ £4,000

1

Which of the following is not a blue cheese?

A: Roquefort

B: Port-Salut

C: Stilton

D: Gorgonzola

2

In which area are unmounted racehorses paraded before the start of a race?

A: Stalls

B: Stable

C: Paddock

D: Traps

3

Which of these cities would be the least likely to host the Commonwealth Games?

A: Toronto

B: Rio de Janeiro

C: Cardiff

D: Auckland

4

Where in the British Isles are the famous TT motorcycle races held annually?

A: Jersey

B: Isle of Man

C: Isle of Wight

D: Anglesey

5

Which of these is a long, low seat without a back, originating from Turkey?

A: Ottoman

B: Dolman

C: Andaman

D: Ealdorman

50:50 Go to page 247   Go to page 259   **?** Answers on page 268

6

In wine terminology, what is meant
by the term 'blancs-de-blancs'?

A: House white wine
B: White wine made from white grapes
C: Superior white wine
D: French grape variety

7

Which of these boxing weight divisions
comes between middle and heavy?

A: Bantam
B: Fly
C: Light
D: Cruiser

8

If you 'cast on' when you begin, and 'cast
off' when you finish, what are you doing?

A: Sailing
B: Knitting
C: Fishing
D: Potting

page
139

9

Which of these is not a type of hammer?

A: Sledge
B: Claw
C: Club
D: Tenon

10

In golf, what name is given to the part
of the fairway surrounding the green?

A: Wrap
B: Shawl
C: Apron
D: Veil

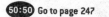 50:50 Go to page 247   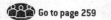 Go to page 259    ? Answers on page 268

7 ◆ £4,000

11

Which of the following terms is used to measure a website's popularity?

- A: Knock
- B: Dent
- C: Hit
- D: Biff

12

From which material is an ice hockey puck made?

- A: Granite
- B: Wood
- C: Rubber
- D: Glass

13

Which of the following moves might you execute whilst bell-ringing?

- A: Front crawl
- B: Backstroke
- C: Butterfly
- D: Breaststroke

14

What does this snooker break add up to: red, green, red, blue, red, black?

- A: 9
- B: 14
- C: 16
- D: 18

15

In which Canadian province or territory is the ski resort of Whistler?

- A: British Columbia
- B: Alberta
- C: Saskatchewan
- D: Yukon

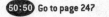 50:50 Go to page 247   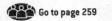 Go to page 259   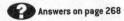 Answers on page 268

7 ◆ £4,000

16

Which of these is a Turkish pastry filled with nuts and honey?

◆A: Baklava
◆B: Barquettes
◆C: Halva
◆D: Panforte

17

In which country was the tennis star Gabriela Sabatini born?

◆A: Italy
◆B: Argentina
◆C: Spain
◆D: Brazil

18

Which of these distances is also run over hurdles in the Olympic Games?

◆A: 200 metres
◆B: 400 metres
◆C: 800 metres
◆D: 1500 metres

19

Who captained the European golf team in the 2002 Ryder Cup?

◆A: Tony Jacklin
◆B: Sam Torrance
◆C: Seve Ballesteros
◆D: Bernard Gallacher

20

Which national museum can be found at Beaulieu in Hampshire?

◆A: National Folk Museum
◆B: National Motor Museum
◆C: National Maritime Museum
◆D: British Museum

 50:50 Go to page 247    Go to page 259   ❓ Answers on page 268

7 ◆ £4,000

21

Cider vats are traditionally made from which wood?

A: Elm

B: Beech

C: Oak

D: Apple

22

In horse racing, what term is used to refer to a horse which has not yet won a race?

A: Rookie

B: Amateur

C: Novice

D: Tenderfoot

23

page **142**

Of which sport is the IAAF the governing body?

A: Athletics

B: American Football

C: Association Football

D: Formula One

24

With which sport is New Zealand's Jonah Lomu chiefly associated?

A: Cricket

B: Rugby Union

C: Golf

D: Tennis

25

Which of these would be mostly likely to suffer from 'the bends'?

A: Circus clown

B: Trapeze artist

C: Scuba diver

D: Gymnast

 50:50 Go to page 247   Go to page 259   Answers on page 268

7 ◆ £4,000

26

Skeets and clays are used in
a discipline of which of these sports?

A: Archery
B: Shooting
C: Fencing
D: Curling

27

By doing which of the following can baseball
players slowly advance round the bases?

A: Robbing
B: Plundering
C: Swiping
D: Stealing

28

Which 3,000 metre runner famously tripped over Zola
Budd's leg in the 1984 Los Angeles Olympic Games?

page
143

A: Florence Griffith-Joyner
B: Marion Jones
C: Mary Decker-Slaney
D: Valerie Brisco-Hooks

29

With which sport is Jürgen
Klinsmann chiefly associated?

A: Tennis
B: Cricket
C: Football
D: Golf

30

A new version of which of these British
cars appeared on Britain's roads in 2001?

A: Mini Cooper
B: Reliant Robin
C: Ford Capri
D: Morris Minor

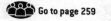 50:50 Go to page 247   Go to page 259   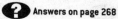 ? Answers on page 268

7 ◆ £4,000

31

Which Scottish football club has its home ground at Ibrox Stadium?

- A: Glasgow Rangers
- B: Motherwell
- C: Aberdeen
- D: Dundee

32

What name is given to a circular embroidery frame?

- A: Hoop
- B: Circle
- C: Wheel
- D: Orb

33

Which country did Olga Korbut represent when she won a gymnastics gold medal at the Munich Olympics?

- A: USSR
- B: Hungary
- C: Switzerland
- D: USA

34

In which sport did Rachel Heyhoe-Flint captain England?

- A: Sailing
- B: Cricket
- C: Croquet
- D: Netball

35

Which jockey rode Aldaniti to victory in the 1981 Grand National?

- A: Willie Carson
- B: Bob Champion
- C: Lester Piggott
- D: Pat Eddery

50:50 Go to page 247   Go to page 259   ? Answers on page 268

7 ♦ £4,000

36

In which of these sports might you hit a 'fly ball'?

- A: Golf
- B: Cricket
- C: Tennis
- D: Baseball

37

What did Muhammad Ali refuse to do that caused him to be stripped of his world boxing title?

- A: Join the army
- B: Fight a challenger
- C: Lose weight
- D: Change his name

38

Which term is generally used to mean a folder in which incoming e-mail is stored on a computer?

page 145

- A: E-tray
- B: Postfile
- C: Inbox
- D: Letterbox

39

What sort of sauce would accompany a main dish described as 'mornay'?

- A: Bolognese
- B: Cheese
- C: Brown
- D: Tomato

40

Which of the following is a bogey in golf?

- A: One under par
- B: Hole in one
- C: One over par
- D: Two over par

 50:50 Go to page 247   Go to page 259   ? Answers on page 268

41

In motoring terms, for what does
the abbreviation GTi stand?

A: Gearbox Transmission Intelligence

B: Gran Tourismo Injection

C: Global Tracking Indicator

D: Gasoline Turbo Injection

42

The racecourse at Sandown Park is in which county?

A: Sussex

B: Hampshire

C: Berkshire

D: Surrey

43

Which of the following colours is not
used in British electricity flex or cable?

A: Red

B: Orange

C: Yellow & Green

D: Blue

44

How many pockets are there on
a standard sized billiard table?

A: 4

B: 6

C: 8

D: 10

45

Which of these terms refers to the narrow
side of the pitch in relation to a rugby scrum?

A: Blindside

B: Shortside

C: Outside

D: Nearside

50:50 Go to page 247　　👥 Go to page 259　　❓ Answers on page 268

7 ◆ £4,000

46

Which of these sports is played on an oval field?

A: American Football
B: Association Football
C: Australian Rules Football
D: Canadian Football

47

In which European country is
the Monza motor racing circuit?

A: Italy
B: Spain
C: France
D: Germany

48

Which of the following is the
name of a gymnastic discipline?

A: Lyrical
B: Prosodic
C: Rhythmic
D: Iambic

49

Which material is used to seal joints in masonry?

A: Cannon
B: Grapeshot
C: Cordite
D: Mortar

50

Useful in DIY, what do the initials MDF stand for?

A: Maximum dye fast
B: Medium-density fibreboard
C: Minimum detectable force
D: Member of Decorator's Federation

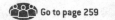 50:50 Go to page 247   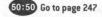 Go to page 259   ? Answers on page 268

7 ◆ £4,000

51

Which of these Scots needs a set of wheels to compete in their chosen sport?

- A: Colin Montgomerie
- B: David Coulthard
- C: Rhona Martin
- D: Gary McAllister

52

Fatima Whitbread was a champion in which event?

- A: 100 metres
- B: Diving
- C: Javelin
- D: Pole vault

53

Which of these cities has not hosted the summer Olympics twice?

- A: Paris
- B: London
- C: Los Angeles
- D: Montreal

54

In classical mythology, who was the god of wine?

- A: Jupiter
- B: Mars
- C: Bacchus
- D: Vulcan

55

Which sport takes its name from the French for a bishop's crozier or staff?

- A: Boules
- B: Pelota
- C: Pétanque
- D: Lacrosse

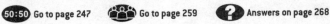 50:50 Go to page 247   Go to page 259   ? Answers on page 268

7 ◆ £4,000

56

With which motorsport is Colin McRae associated?

A: Formula One
B: Speedway
C: Superbikes
D: Rallying

57

Which of these is a capturing move in chess?

A: En passant
B: En courant
C: En bloc
D: En brosse

58

Who won the 2002 US Masters golf tournament?

page
149

A: Phil Mickelson
B: Tiger Woods
C: Vijay Singh
D: Ben Crenshaw

59

In which sport was John Francome a champion seven times from 1976-1985?

A: Motor racing
B: Motorcycle racing
C: Horse racing
D: Powerboat racing

60

In cooking, which word means to immerse briefly in boiling water?

A: Blush
B: Blanch
C: Pale
D: Bleach

7 ◆ £4,000

61

Which English Premiership club won the 2002 FA Cup Final?

- A: Manchester United
- B: Chelsea
- C: Arsenal
- D: Newcastle United

62

Where would you normally wear espadrilles?

- A: On your head
- B: On your shoulders
- C: Around your waist
- D: On your feet

63

Scottish, Lakeland and West Highland White are all breeds of which dog?

- A: Poodle
- B: Spaniel
- C: Terrier
- D: Corgi

64

Which famous fair is held in Nottingham every year?

- A: Swan
- B: Goose
- C: Duck
- D: Chicken

50:50 Go to page 247 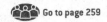 Go to page 259  Answers on page 268

15	**£1 MILLION**
14	£500,000
13	£250,000
12	£125,000
11	£64,000
10	**£32,000**
9	£16,000
8 ◆	**£8,000**
7 ◇	£4,000
6 ◆	£2,000
5 ◆	**£1,000**
4 ◆	£500
3 ◆	£300
2 ◆	£200
1 ◆	£100

8 ◆ £8,000

1

Which is a technique for ornamenting silver?

A: Pursuing

B: Tracking

C: Chasing

D: Coursing

2

How many points does a darts player need to score if they are left needing double top?

A: 50

B: 40

C: 30

D: 20

3

Which of the following sports was banned in Scotland by James II in 1457 because it interfered with the practice of archery?

A: Cricket

B: Golf

C: Football

D: Jousting

4

What name is given to the partner that accompanies a deep-sea diver?

A: Chum

B: Pal

C: Mate

D: Buddy

5

Collage comes from the French word for what?

A: Tape

B: Glue

C: Thread

D: Paper

50:50 Go to page 248   Go to page 260   ? Answers on page 268

8 ◆ £8,000

Which of these golfers is nicknamed 'Supermex'?

A: Arnold Palmer
B: Jack Nicklaus
C: Gary Player
D: Lee Trevino

7

Ornithology is the scientific term for which pastime?

A: Bird-watching
B: Stamp collecting
C: Juggling
D: Trainspotting

8

Which of these is a difficult cricket delivery?

A: Stoker
B: Yorker
C: Dealer
D: Bather

9

With which sport is Spain's
Miguel Induráin chiefly associated?

A: Motor racing
B: Cycling
C: Tennis
D: Golf

10

Which part of a plant produces pollen?

A: Calyx
B: Anther
C: Petal
D: Sepal

50:50 Go to page 248   Go to page 260   ? Answers on page 268

11

For which team have the brothers Steve and Mark Waugh played test cricket?

A: Australia

B: New Zealand

C: South Africa

D: West Indies

12

In which country are the famous ski resorts of Kitzbühel, Übergurgl and St Anton?

A: Andorra

B: Switzerland

C: France

D: Austria

13

In international rugby union, how many points are awarded for a try?

A: 2

B: 3

C: 4

D: 5

14

Apart from Stoke City, for which other English club did Stanley Matthews play professional football?

A: Bolton Wanderers

B: Blackburn Rovers

C: Burnley

D: Blackpool

15

In which city is the Clifton Suspension Bridge?

A: Birmingham

B: Bristol

C: Manchester

D: London

50:50 Go to page 248   Go to page 260   ? Answers on page 268

8 ◆ £8,000

16

In computer and digital systems, what name is given to a group of four bits otherwise known as half a byte?

- A: Peck
- B: Nibble
- C: Pick
- D: Cram

17

In which year did rugby's Five Nations Championship become the Six Nations?

- A: 1995
- B: 1997
- C: 2000
- D: 2002

18

Which theme park can be found two miles outside the town of Windsor?

- A: Alton Towers
- B: Blackpool
- C: Legoland
- D: Chessington

19

In 2001, which men's tennis player became the youngest ever to top the ATP rankings?

- A: Lleyton Hewitt
- B: Marat Safin
- C: Gustavo Kuerten
- D: Carlos Moya

20

Which of these would the American sportsman 'Mo' Greene normally use?

- A: Pit crew
- B: Baseball bat
- C: Safety helmet
- D: Running shoes

50:50 Go to page 248 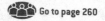 Go to page 260 **?** Answers on page 268

8 ◆ £8,000

21

William Henry Fox Talbot was a pioneer in which field?

- A: Photography
- B: Ballroom dancing
- C: Magazine editing
- D: Weaving

22

Which wood was traditionally used to make longbows?

- A: Yew
- B: Willow
- C: Oak
- D: Apple

23

Who was England's goalkeeper in the 1966 World Cup final winning side?

- A: Gordon Banks
- B: Peter Bonetti
- C: Alex Stepney
- D: Peter Shilton

24

From which occupation did ice dance champion Christopher Dean resign to concentrate on skating?

- A: Policeman
- B: Salesman
- C: Insurance agent
- D: Builder

25

Complete the name of the American football team, the Green Bay ...?

- A: Packers
- B: Labourers
- C: Dockers
- D: Porters

50:50 Go to page 248   Go to page 260   ? Answers on page 268

8 ◆ £8,000

26

In which country was the Olympic long-distance runner Haile Gebreselassie born?

- A: Congo
- B: Ethiopia
- C: Somalia
- D: Zimbabwe

27

In which year did Damon Hill win the Formula One world motor racing championship?

- A: 1988
- B: 1990
- C: 1996
- D: 1998

28

Which of the following is the equivalent of the Davis Cup for women tennis players?

- A: Association Cup
- B: Alliance Cup
- C: Fed Cup
- D: Corporation Cup

29

What is the nationality of the former Olympic gymnast Nadia Comaneci?

- A: Hungarian
- B: Russian
- C: Romanian
- D: Polish

30

Which country won the 1999 Cricket World Cup?

- A: Sri Lanka
- B: Pakistan
- C: South Africa
- D: Australia

50:50 Go to page 248 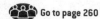 Go to page 260  Answers on page 268

8 ◆ £8,000

31

Which football club is not nicknamed after a colour?

- A: Manchester City
- B: Liverpool
- C: Leeds United
- D: Everton

32

The biathlon consists of rifle shooting and which other sport?

- A: Cycling
- B: Cross-country skiing
- C: Swimming
- D: Running

33

Which country won the first rugby union World Cup in 1987?

- A: France
- B: England
- C: Australia
- D: New Zealand

34

Which member of European royalty competed in the bobsleigh event in the 2002 Winter Olympics?

- A: King Juan Carlos
- B: Prince Albert of Monaco
- C: Prince Carl Philip of Sweden
- D: Prince Harry

35

For which country did the famous all-rounder Kapil Dev play test cricket?

- A: India
- B: Australia
- C: Pakistan
- D: South Africa

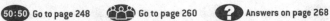

50:50 Go to page 248   Go to page 260   ? Answers on page 268

8 ◆ £8,000

36

On what date is Burn's Night celebrated?

- A: Dec 25th
- B: Jan 25th
- C: Feb 25th
- D: March 25th

37

At which sport would spectators be likely to watch from the 'Silver Ring'?

- A: Boxing
- B: Ice hockey
- C: Tennis
- D: Horse racing

38

Which snooker term is used to describe the area at the top of the table marked by a line where players often attempt to position the cue-ball?

- A: Foil
- B: Baffle
- C: Baulk
- D: Stymie

39

Which American Football team won the 2002 Super Bowl?

- A: Dallas Cowboys
- B: Denver Broncos
- C: New England Patriots
- D: Buffalo Bills

40

What was the former name of Australian cricket's Pura Milk Cup?

- A: Sheffield Shield
- B: Preston Plate
- C: Manchester Medal
- D: Rotherham Ribbon

50:50 Go to page 248   Go to page 260   **?** Answers on page 268
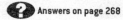

8 ◆ £8,000

41

Which football club moved to the St Mary's Stadium for the start of the 2001-2002 season?

- A: Huddersfield Town
- B: Fulham
- C: Norwich City
- D: Southampton

42

In the context of wine, what is the literal meaning of the term 'cru' as in 'grand cru'?

- A: Grape
- B: Taste
- C: Year
- D: Growth

43

Which of these is a type of Greek pastry manufactured in wafer-thin sheets?

- A: Shortcrust pastry
- B: Choux pastry
- C: Filo pastry
- D: Strudel pastry

44

In international rugby union, what number shirt does the fullback normally wear?

- A: 1
- B: 9
- C: 11
- D: 15

45

For which country did Basil D'Oliveira play test cricket in the 1960s?

- A: England
- B: South Africa
- C: Australia
- D: New Zealand

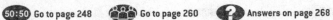

50:50 Go to page 248   Go to page 260   ? Answers on page 268

46

Which of the following is the highest possible scoring word in the English language version of Scrabble?

- A: Quartzy
- B: Bezique
- C: Cazique
- D: Squawky

47

What is the home ground of Stoke City FC?

- A: Britannia Stadium
- B: Guinea Stadium
- C: Pound Stadium
- D: Groat Stadium

48

Which of these is a type of bowling green?

page **161**

- A: Tiara
- B: Crown
- C: Sceptre
- D: Garland

49

In which of these London attractions would you find the Round Reading Room?

- A: British Library
- B: Victoria and Albert Museum
- C: Science Museum
- D: British Museum

50

After whom is the 'Man of the Match' award for rugby league's Challenge Cup Final named?

- A: Colin Todd
- B: Lance Todd
- C: Bob Todd
- D: Sweeney Todd

50:50 Go to page 248   Go to page 260   **?** Answers on page 268

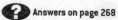

8 ◆ £8,000

51

Which of the following is a long, looping pass to a receiver in American football?

A: Bomb
B: Torpedo
C: Grenade
D: Rocket

52

In which year were the Berlin summer Olympic Games cancelled?

A: 1916
B: 1920
C: 1940
D: 1948

53

Who was the youngest person in the 20th century to win a tennis Grand Slam title?

A: Chris Evert
B: Martina Hingis
C: Jana Novotna
D: Venus Williams

54

Which of these would you find in York?

A: National Seafarers' Museum
B: National Railway Museum
C: National Portrait Gallery
D: National Photographic Archive

55

What was the regular fielding position of legendary cricketer Godfrey Evans?

A: Mid off
B: Long leg
C: Gully
D: Wicket-keeper

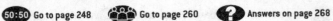

50:50 Go to page 248   Go to page 260   Answers on page 268

8 ◆ £8,000

56

In which field is Welsh rugby legend
J P R Williams a qualified practitioner?

- A: Law
- B: Medicine
- C: Architecture
- D: Accountancy

57

In Australian Rules Football, you can score
6 points for a goal and 1 point for a... what?

- A: Bum
- B: Bottom
- C: Derriere
- D: Behind

58

Which country's Formula One Grand Prix takes
place around the streets of its capital city?

- A: UK
- B: Italy
- C: Germany
- D: Monaco

59

The ancient Incan ruins of Machu
Picchu are in which country?

- A: Argentina
- B: Spain
- C: Nicaragua
- D: Peru

60

Which of these prestigious races did
Mike Hailwood win seven times?

- A: Le Mans 24-Hour Race
- B: Isle of Man TT Senior
- C: Monte Carlo Rally
- D: Indianapolis 500

50:50 Go to page 248   Go to page 260   Answers on page 268

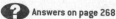

50:50		

15	**£1 MILLION**
14	£500,000
13	£250,000
12	£125,000
11	£64,000
10	**£32,000**
9 ◆	**£16,000**
8 ◆	£8,000
7 ◆	£4,000
6 ◆	£2,000
5 ◆	**£1,000**
4 ◆	£500
3 ◆	£300
2 ◆	£200
1 ◆	£100

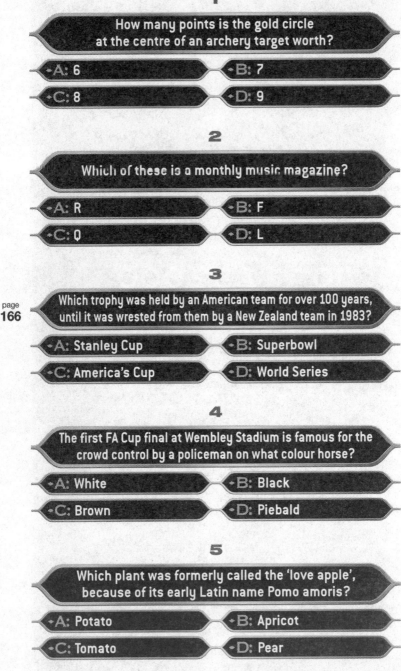

1

How many points is the gold circle
at the centre of an archery target worth?

A: 6
B: 7
C: 8
D: 9

2

Which of these is a monthly music magazine?

A: R
B: F
C: Q
D: L

3

Which trophy was held by an American team for over 100 years,
until it was wrested from them by a New Zealand team in 1983?

A: Stanley Cup
B: Superbowl
C: America's Cup
D: World Series

4

The first FA Cup final at Wembley Stadium is famous for the
crowd control by a policeman on what colour horse?

A: White
B: Black
C: Brown
D: Piebald

5

Which plant was formerly called the 'love apple',
because of its early Latin name Pomo amoris?

A: Potato
B: Apricot
C: Tomato
D: Pear

50:50 Go to page 248　　Go to page 260　　? Answers on page 268

9 ◆ £16,000

6

Where is the finishing line of the London Marathon?

A: Oxford Circus
B: Regents Park
C: The Mall
D: Marble Arch

7

Which British fashion designer, born in 1969, was dubbed an 'enfant terrible' by the fashion press?

A: John Galliano
B: Stella McCartney
C: Alexander McQueen
D: Paul Smith

8

Which famous sporting venue is near Towcester, Northamptonshire?

A: Silverstone
B: Brands Hatch
C: Brooklands
D: Mallory Park

9

What name is given to the Italian dessert made from sponge soaked in coffee and Marsala wine, and topped with soft cheese and powdered chocolate?

A: Zabaglione
B: Cassata
C: Tiramisu
D: Mascarpone

10

Which former England footballer married Joy of the Beverley Sisters singing group?

A: Stanley Matthews
B: Billy Wright
C: Tom Finney
D: Frank Swift

50:50 Go to page 248    Go to page 260   **?** Answers on page 268

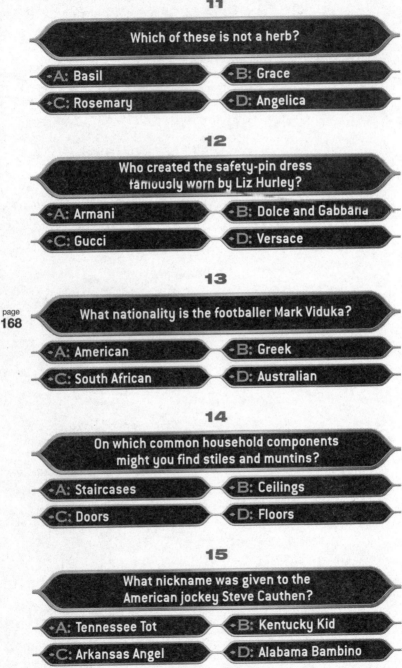

11

Which of these is not a herb?

- A: Basil
- B: Grace
- C: Rosemary
- D: Angelica

12

Who created the safety-pin dress famously worn by Liz Hurley?

- A: Armani
- B: Dolce and Gabbana
- C: Gucci
- D: Versace

13

What nationality is the footballer Mark Viduka?

- A: American
- B: Greek
- C: South African
- D: Australian

14

On which common household components might you find stiles and muntins?

- A: Staircases
- B: Ceilings
- C: Doors
- D: Floors

15

What nickname was given to the American jockey Steve Cauthen?

- A: Tennessee Tot
- B: Kentucky Kid
- C: Arkansas Angel
- D: Alabama Bambino

50:50 Go to page 248   Go to page 260   ? Answers on page 268

9 ◆ £16,000

16

Hollie Point is an English speciality of which craft?

- A: Tapestry
- B: Lace-making
- C: Silkscreen printing
- D: Quilting

17

In which of these sports would you be likely to compete in the K1 or K2 class?

- A: Showjumping
- B: Canoeing
- C: Skiing
- D: Judo

18

Which motor car manufacturer makes a model called the Almera?

- A: Honda
- B: Nissan
- C: Daewoo
- D: Toyota

19

In Australia, by what popular name is Perth's leading cricket ground known?

- A: GABBA
- B: QUACA
- C: WACA
- D: COBBER

20

What name is given to the encoding of information before it is sent over the Internet?

- A: Ciphering
- B: Encryption
- C: Scrambling
- D: Camouflage

 50:50 Go to page 248   Go to page 261    ? Answers on page 268

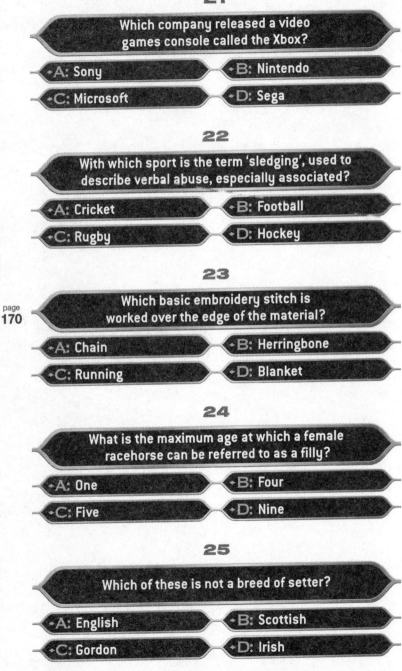

21

Which company released a video games console called the Xbox?

A: Sony

B: Nintendo

C: Microsoft

D: Sega

22

With which sport is the term 'sledging', used to describe verbal abuse, especially associated?

A: Cricket

B: Football

C: Rugby

D: Hockey

23

Which basic embroidery stitch is worked over the edge of the material?

A: Chain

B: Herringbone

C: Running

D: Blanket

24

What is the maximum age at which a female racehorse can be referred to as a filly?

A: One

B: Four

C: Five

D: Nine

25

Which of these is not a breed of setter?

A: English

B: Scottish

C: Gordon

D: Irish

50:50 Go to page 249   Go to page 261   **?** Answers on page 268

9 ◆ £16,000

26

By what name are horizontal blinds more commonly known?

A: German blinds
B: Austrian blinds
C: Venetian blinds
D: Roman blinds

27

Which British Olympic athlete refused to run on a Sunday due to his religious beliefs?

A: Eric Liddell
B: Harold Abrahams
C: Albert Hill
D: Charles Clibbon

28

Which former England wicketkeeper also pursues a career as an artist?

page 171

A: Allan Knott
B: Bob Taylor
C: Godfrey Evans
D: Jack Russell

29

What name is given to the string of a kite?

A: Bridle
B: Shackle
C: Tether
D: Rein

30

Which of these is the slang name given to the area outside the three point arc on a basketball court?

A: Midtown
B: Uptown
C: Downtown
D: Outtatown

50:50 Go to page 249 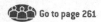 Go to page 261  Answers on page 268

9 ◆ £16,000

31

Which of these is a two-wheeled carriage used in horse and trap racing?

- A: Testy
- B: Crabby
- C: Sullen
- D: Sulky

32

In computer terminology, what is denoted by .ac.uk in an Internet domain name?

- A: Accounting
- B: Actual
- C: Academic
- D: Accredited

33

On which British golf course is the Old Course situated in the Eden Estuary?

- A: Royal Troon
- B: Muirfield
- C: St Andrews
- D: Turnberry

34

What is the predominant colour of the home shirts of Burnley, Aston Villa and West Ham United football clubs?

- A: Green
- B: Claret
- C: Yellow
- D: White

35

Which of these is the projecting moulding at the top of tall pieces of antique furniture?

- A: Cornice
- B: Niche
- C: Capital
- D: Pediment

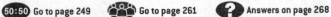
50:50 Go to page 249   Go to page 261   ? Answers on page 268

9 ◆ £16,000

36

How many balls are used in pool, including the cue ball?

- A: 22
- B: 16
- C: 14
- D: 24

37

Which British fashion designer opened her first shop called 'Let It Rock' in the King's Road in the 1970s?

- A: Zandra Rhodes
- B: Mary Quant
- C: Jean Muir
- D: Vivienne Westwood

38

What was the nickname of 1950s tennis star Gussie Moran?

- A: Gorgeous
- B: Graceful
- C: Glamorous
- D: Gadding

39

If you purchased an antique kelim, what would you be buying?

- A: Musket
- B: Vase
- C: Chaise longue
- D: Rug

40

Which of these is a Malaysian car manufacturer?

- A: Electron
- B: Neutron
- C: Proton
- D: Nucleus

50:50 Go to page 249 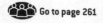 Go to page 261  Answers on page 268

9 ◆ £16,000

41

From which English football club was Eric Cantona transferred to Manchester United in 1992?

A: Leeds United

B: Liverpool

C: Everton

D: Blackburn Rovers

42

What is the distinguishing feature of the breed of domestic cat known as the Scottish Fold?

A: It has wrinkly legs

B: It has a curly tail

C: It has folds of skin over its eyes

D: Its ears are folded forward

43

What did Captain Matthew Webb do on August 24th-25th 1875?

A: Climb the Matterhorn

B: Swim the English channel

C: Walk from London to Edinburgh

D: Run 10 marathons

44

At which distance did Sebastian Coe win an Olympic gold medal in 1980?

A: 400 metres

B: 800 metres

C: 1500 metres

D: 5000 metres

45

What is the nationality of the entrepreneur and beautician Estée Lauder?

A: Belgian

B: French

C: American

D: Canadian

 50:50 Go to page 249   Go to page 261   Answers on page 268

9 ◆ £16,000

46

Michael Parkinson and 'Dickie' Bird both support which football team?

- A: Huddersfield Town
- B: Sheffield Wednesday
- C: Leeds United
- D: Barnsley

47

Which champion jockey rode into history by winning all seven races on the card at Ascot in September 1996?

- A: Pat Eddery
- B: Frankie Dettori
- C: Willie Carson
- D: Kieran Fallon

48

What is batik?

page
175

- A: Form of basketry
- B: Method of dyeing fabric
- C: Style of bell-ringing
- D: Way of bird-watching

49

Which snooker player compiled a 147 maximum break in just five minutes and twenty seconds in the 1997 Embassy World Championship?

- A: Stephen Hendry
- B: Jimmy White
- C: Ronnie O'Sullivan
- D: Paul Hunter

50

Which of the following Olympic events is contested solely by men?

- A: Decathlon
- B: Shot put
- C: Hammer throw
- D: Pentathlon

50:50 Go to page 249   Go to page 261   ? Answers on page 268

51

Mosta, Qom, and Valetta are
all on which holiday island?

A: Malta
B: Cyprus
C: Crete
D: Tenerife

52

In which of these sports might
you execute a 'flying mare'?

A: Fly fishing
B: Wrestling
C: Canoeing
D: Show jumping

53

Of which rugby club did former England star
Rob Andrew become a director in 1995?

A: Wasps
B: Saracens
C: Newcastle
D: Harlequins

54

On which US city was the board
game 'Monopoly' originally based?

A: Las Vegas
B: New York
C: Atlantic City
D: Chicago

55

What name is given to a single domino?

A: Ivory
B: Bone
C: Marble
D: Wood

50:50 Go to page 249   Go to page 261   ? Answers on page 268

56

Whom did Goran Ivanesevic beat in the final of the 2001 Wimbledon Men's Singles?

- **A: Lleyton Hewitt**
- **B: Pete Sampras**
- **C: Pat Rafter**
- **D: Marat Safin**

50:50 Go to page 249  Go to page 261 **?** Answers on page 268

50:50

15	£1 MILLION
14	£500,000
13	£250,000
12	£125,000
11	£64,000
10 ◆	**£32,000**
9 ◆	£16,000
8 ◆	£8,000
7 ◆	£4,000
6 ◆	£2,000
5 ◆	£1,000
4 ◆	£500
3 ◆	£300
2 ◆	£200
1 ◆	£100

10 ◆ £32,000

1

What colour is a British 13 amp fuse?

A: Red

B: Brown

C: Yellow

D: Black

2

Which British stadium was the venue for the 2002 UEFA Champions' League Final?

A: Millennium Stadium

B: Hampden Park

C: Old Trafford

D: Villa Park

3

Whose design house created the 'Black Pearls' fragrance for women?

A: Cilla Black

B: Elizabeth Taylor

C: Jane Fonda

D: Julia Roberts

4

Which international football team were the first World Cup holders to win the European Championship?

A: Germany

B: Italy

C: England

D: France

5

The Rialto Bridge is a famous tourist attraction in which city?

A: Venice

B: Milan

C: Rome

D: Florence

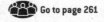 50:50 Go to page 249   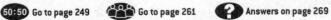 Go to page 261   ? Answers on page 269

10 ◆ £32,000

page
181

6

With which sport are the Australians Roy Emerson and John Newcombe associated?

A: Cricket   B: Rugby Union

C: Golf   D: Tennis

7

Which breed of terrier takes its name from a character in the Sir Walter Scott novel 'Guy Mannering'?

A: Sealyham   B: Kerry Blue

C: Dandie Dinmont   D: Jack Russell

8

In which country is Eden Gardens a famous international cricket venue?

A: Australia   B: Sri Lanka

C: India   D: New Zealand

9

What colour is the ball used in a standard game of roulette?

A: Yellow   B: Black

C: White   D: Red

10

For which team did Nigel Mansell drive when he won the Formula One World Drivers' Championship?

A: McLaren   B: Williams

C: Ferrari   D: Benetton

50:50 Go to page 249   Go to page 261   ? Answers on page 269

10 ◆ £32,000

11

By whom was Henry Cooper controversially
beaten in his last professional fight?

A: Joe Bugner
B: Muhammad Ali
C: Brian London
D: Joe Frazier

12

In which event in the 2002 Winter Olympics were the runners-up awarded
a set of duplicate gold medals after revelations about a judge's voting?

A: Figure skating
B: Downhill skiing
C: Snowboarding
D: Curling

13

Which of the following horse racing
terms is betting slang for 3-1?

A: Curtains
B: Floorboards
C: Carpet
D: Wallpaper

14

How many pieces does each player
start with in a game of draughts?

A: 8
B: 10
C: 12
D: 14

15

Which of these England cricketers was the
first to be knighted for his services to the game?

A: Ted Dexter
B: Len Hutton
C: Jack Hobbs
D: Colin Cowdrey

50:50 Go to page 249   Go to page 261   ? Answers on page 269

10 ◆ £32,000

16

Which woman was the first to win the tennis Grand Slam?

A: Maureen Connolly
B: Maria Bueno
C: Billie Jean King
D: Margaret Court

17

From which country does the red table wine Bull's Blood originate?

A: Germany
B: Hungary
C: Austria
D: Spain

18

In which country is the famous Naas racecourse?

page
183

A: USA
B: Republic of Ireland
C: UK
D: Australia

19

How many Wimbledon men's singles titles did John McEnroe win?

A: 1
B: 2
C: 3
D: 4

20

In which year did Nick Faldo win his first Open golf championship?

A: 1983
B: 1985
C: 1987
D: 1989

 50:50 Go to page 249   Go to page 261   Answers on page 269

21

What name is given to the known history of an antique object?

A: Origin

B: Derivation

C: Ancestry

D: Provenance

22

In which of these sports might you execute an alley-oop pass?

A: Volleyball

B: Football

C: Basketball

D: Handball

23

Which cyclist overcame cancer to win his third successive Tour de France in 2001?

A: Miguel Induráin

B: David Millar

C: Lance Armstrong

D: Jan Ullrich

24

With which sport is fashion designer Teddy Tinling chiefly associated?

A: Ice dancing

B: Skiing

C: Tennis

D: Athletics

25

Camogie is which country's native field sport for women?

A: France

B: Ireland

C: Spain

D: Italy

50:50 Go to page 249   Go to page 261   ? Answers on page 269

26

Which cricketer played football for Arsenal and England, and cricket for Middlesex and England?

- A: Len Hutton
- B: Dennis Compton
- C: Tom Graveney
- D: Brian Statham

27

What name is given to the first firing of a newly made clay pot?

- A: Pastry
- B: Cookie
- C: Shortcake
- D: Biscuit

28

In which of Britain's National Parks is the peak of Cader Idris?

- A: North York Moors
- B: Peak District
- C: Lake District
- D: Snowdonia

29

What name is given to a creamy mixture of clay with water?

- A: Trip
- B: Slip
- C: Slide
- D: Spill

30

In which athletics event was Olympic gold medallist Ed Moses unbeaten, from August 1977 to June 1987?

- A: 100 metres
- B: 200 metres
- C: 400 metres hurdles
- D: 800 metres

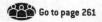 50:50 Go to page 249   Go to page 261    ? Answers on page 269

31

How many numbers appear
on a standard UK bingo card?

- A: 10
- B: 15
- C: 20
- D: 25

32

Which of the following is an aerial
manouevre in windsurfing?

- A: Cheese roll
- B: Bacon sandwich
- C: Chip butty
- D: Toasted cheese

33

Which of these snooker players has been
nicknamed the 'Wizard of Wishaw'?

- A: Stephen Hendry
- B: John Higgins
- C: Alan McManus
- D: Mark Williams

34

Marigolds belong to which family of plants?

- A: Rose
- B: Daisy
- C: Tulip
- D: Primrose

35

Which of the following was voted
Top Gear Car of the Year in 2002?

- A: Audi TT
- B: Range Rover
- C: Peugeot 307
- D: Fiat Multipla

50:50 Go to page 249 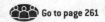 Go to page 261  Answers on page 269

10 ◆ £32,000

36

Which was the first Asian city to host the summer Olympic Games?

- A: Seoul
- B: Hong Kong
- C: Beijing
- D: Tokyo

37

Which of these is a computing facility used to eliminate messages from unwanted users?

- A: Bozo filter
- B: Dummy partition
- C: Idiot screen
- D: Zombie wall

38

Which of these is not a 2002 Super League rugby club?

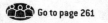page **187**

- A: Wigan Warriors
- B: Watford Hornets
- C: Widnes Vikings
- D: Warrington Wolves

39

In which sport is a Madison event contested?

- A: Archery
- B: Skiing
- C: Cycling
- D: Fencing

40

Which country do the Great Britain and Ireland team play in golf's biennial Walker Cup?

- A: Canada
- B: Australia
- C: New Zealand
- D: USA

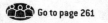

50:50 Go to page 249   Go to page 261   **?** Answers on page 269

10 ◆ £32,000

41

At which sport do ladies compete in the annual Evian Masters?

- A: Tennis
- B: Darts
- C: Badminton
- D: Golf

42

Which actor is co-owner with Carl Haas of an Indy Car racing team in the USA?

- A: James Garner
- B: Paul Newman
- C: Robert Redford
- D: Dustin Hoffman

43

In Italian footballing terminology, what is catenaccio?

- A: Referee
- B: Defensive style of play
- C: Offside rule
- D: Penalty kick

44

Which of these is a computing term referring to the exchange of data between two devices?

- A: Nod
- B: Wink
- C: Handshake
- D: High five

45

At which sport did Ian Preece become world amateur champion in 1999?

- A: Tennis
- B: Snooker
- C: Boxing
- D: Archery

 50:50 Go to page 250   Go to page 262   ? Answers on page 269

10 ◆ £32,000

46

Which Irish rugby union club gave its name to
the tactic also known as the 'up and under'?

- A: Cork Constitution
- B: Garryowen
- C: Shannon
- D: Young Munster

47

Before he changed his name to Muhammad Ali,
what was Cassius Clay's middle name?

- A: Martin
- B: Malcolm
- C: Michael
- D: Marcellus

48

Which term, important to fishermen, describes
anything inhabiting or situated on a riverbank?

- A: Agrarian
- B: Aquarian
- C: Riparian
- D: Vivarium

49

The name of which flowering plant
comes from the Latin meaning 'I wash'?

- A: Lily
- B: Lupin
- C: Lavender
- D: Lilac

50

Which popular cake was named in honour of the marriage
of Princess Victoria, a granddaughter of Queen Victoria?

- A: Stollen
- B: Strudel
- C: Battenberg
- D: Sachertorte

 50:50 Go to page 250   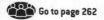 Go to page 262    Answers on page 269

51

In which sport is the Corbillon Cup a major competition?

A: Squash

B: Golf

C: Hockey

D: Table tennis

52

Which doll was unveiled for the first time at a 1959 toy fair in New York?

A: Cindy

B: Barbie

C: Tiny Tears

D: Bye-lo Baby

50:50 Go to page 250   Go to page 262   ? Answers on page 269

15	**£1 MILLION**
14	£500,000
13	£250,000
12	£125,000
11 ◆	**£64,000**
10 ◆	**£32,000**
9 ◆	£16,000
8 ◆	£8,000
7 ◆	£4,000
6 ◆	£2,000
5 ◆	**£1,000**
4 ◆	£500
3 ◆	£300
2 ◆	£200
1 ◆	£100

1

In which British coastal town does
the annual Fastnet yachting race finish?

A: Portsmouth   B: Plymouth

C: Cowes   D: Southampton

2

How much income tax has to be paid in a standard game
of 'Monopoly' if you land on the appropriate square?

A: £50   B: £100

C: £150   D: £200

3

Which former jockey's middle names are Hunter Fisher?

A: Steve Cauthen B: Willie Carson

C: Lester Piggott D: Walter Swinburn

4

What was the nationality of the legendary
long distance runner Paavo Nurmi?

A: Swedish   B: Danish

C: Norwegian   D: Finnish

5

In the world of pigeon racing,
what are baby pigeons called?

A: Squeakers   B: Squealers

C: Squawkers   D: Squirmers

50:50 Go to page 250 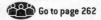 Go to page 262 Answers on page 269

6

Which is the final event of an Olympic decathlon competition?

- A: 400 metres
- B: Shot put
- C: 1500 metres
- D: Pole vault

7

What is the nickname of the Australian national association football team?

- A: Wombats
- B: Emus
- C: Footyboys
- D: Socceroos

8

Which of these is a method of embroidery, in which material of one kind or colour is cut and sewn to another?

page 193

- A: Macramé
- B: Collage
- C: Appliqué
- D: Tapestry

9

Whom did Lennox Lewis beat in the final to win the 1988 Olympic super-heavyweight boxing gold medal?

- A: George Foreman
- B: Tyrell Biggs
- C: Riddick Bowe
- D: Ray Mercer

10

In which sport is a competitor most likely to use a 'spray skirt'?

- A: Cycling
- B: Water skiing
- C: Canoeing
- D: Golf

50:50 Go to page 250 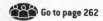 Go to page 262 **?** Answers on page 269

11

Which of the following is not an event in horse racing's Triple Crown in the USA?

- A: Kentucky Derby
- B: Tennessee Gold Cup
- C: Preakness Stakes
- D: Belmont Stakes

12

For which Formula One racing team did Jensen Button drive in the 2002 season?

- A: Jordan
- B: Ferrari
- C: Minardi
- D: Renault

13

In which country is the Gabba a test cricket venue?

- A: New Zealand
- B: South Africa
- C: Australia
- D: Zimbabwe

14

Who was the first British player to win the Wimbledon Women's Singles title after WWII?

- A: Ann Jones
- B: Virginia Wade
- C: Christine Truman
- D: Angela Mortimer

15

In which sport are the Barcelona Dragons, Scottish Claymores and Frankfurt Galaxy top European teams?

- A: Ice hockey
- B: Basketball
- C: Baseball
- D: American football

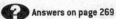
50:50 Go to page 250   Go to page 262   ? Answers on page 269

11 ◆ £64,000

16

What term is used to describe a horse with a golden-coloured coat and silver mane and tail?

A: Palomino

B: Arabian

C: Lippizaner

D: Appaloosa

17

In which US state is the Badlands National Park?

A: Nebraska

B: Montana

C: Kansas

D: South Dakota

18

In 2001, American men won three of golf's four 'Majors': what nationality is Retief Goosen, the winner of the US Open that year?

A: Danish

B: Zimbabwean

C: Swedish

D: South African

19

In which English city is the Odsal Stadium?

A: Leeds

B: Bradford

C: Sheffield

D: Nottingham

20

For which English county did test cricketer Alan Knott play?

A: Essex

B: Surrey

C: Sussex

D: Kent

50:50 Go to page 250   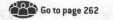 Go to page 262    ? Answers on page 269

11 ◆ £64,000

21

What word means to fail to follow suit to the card led, even if able and required to do so?

- A: Rebut
- B: Revoke
- C: Retract
- D: Renounce

22

Which sport was born following a meeting at the George Hotel, Huddersfield on August 29th 1895?

- A: Pigeon racing
- B: Rugby League
- C: Orienteering
- D: Fell running

23

A Gibson is a classic martini cocktail garnished with what?

- A: Olive
- B: Lemon
- C: Onion
- D: Celery

24

Which former darts world champion was unable to compete for two years due to a condition called 'dartitis'?

- A: John Lowe
- B: Eric Bristow
- C: Jocky Wilson
- D: Bobby George

25

What is the maximum number of clubs a player is allowed in the bag in an official golf tournament?

- A: 10
- B: 12
- C: 14
- D: 16

11 ◆ £64,000

26

Which flowering shrub is known as the 'butterfly bush'?

- A: Daphne
- B: Hebe
- C: Buddleia
- D: Lilac

27

As at the end of the 2001-02 football season, who was the last English manager of Chelsea FC?

- A: Glenn Hoddle
- B: John Hollins
- C: Dave Sexton
- D: Bobby Campbell

28

Which of these cap colours is compulsory for one of the sides in an official water polo match?

page 197

- A: Yellow
- B: Green
- C: Brown
- D: White

29

In which profession has the world-famous athlete Roger Bannister, had a distinguished career?

- A: Heart surgeon
- B: Neurologist
- C: Osteopath
- D: Dentist

30

Which of these is not a breed of terrier?

- A: Wheaten
- B: Bedlington
- C: Airedale
- D: Schnauzer

50:50 Go to page 250   Go to page 262   ? Answers on page 269

31

On which Caribbean island was the
legendary cricketer Sir Gary Sobers born?

◆A: Jamaica   ◆B: Barbados
◆C: Trinidad   ◆D: Grenada

32

Where are the headquarters
of the Automobile Association?

◆A: Southampton   ◆B: Andover
◆C: Basingstoke   ◆D: Slough

33

Which golfer started the final round of the 1996 US Masters
tournament six shots behind the leader but won by five strokes?

◆A: Bernhard Langer   ◆B: Tiger Woods
◆C: Jose Maria Olazabal ◆D: Nick Faldo

34

In which sport was New Zealand's Mark Todd
a gold medalist at the 1984 and 1988 Olympics?

◆A: Rowing   ◆B: Sailing
◆C: Equestrianism ◆D: Fencing

35

Which of these words refers to the informal
system of acceptable behaviour on the Internet?

◆A: Progrocol   ◆B: Netiquette
◆C: Digicorum   ◆D: Webwise

50:50 Go to page 250   Go to page 262   ? Answers on page 269

11 ◆ £64,000

36

Sugar Ray Robinson was world boxing champion at middleweight and which other weight?

A: Welter
B: Light
C: Light heavy
D: Fly

37

Which Arsenal player was voted 2002 PFA Player of the Year?

A: Freddie Ljungberg
B: Patrick Vieira
C: Robert Pires
D: Thierry Henry

38

In which US state is the ski resort of Mammoth?

A: Utah
B: Alaska
C: Vermont
D: California

39

Held at Altcar in Lancashire, in which sport is the Waterloo Cup competed for?

A: Hill walking
B: Whippet racing
C: Hare coursing
D: Crown green bowls

40

Which duke owns Badminton, the venue of the famous horse trials?

A: Duke of Beaufort
B: Duke of Gloucester
C: Duke of Norfolk
D: Duke of Bedford

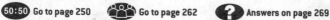 50:50 Go to page 250   Go to page 262   ? Answers on page 269

41

Harold Sakata, who won a silver medal for weightlilfting at the 1948 Olympics, went on to play which James Bond villain?

- A: Dr No
- B: Goldfinger
- C: Scaramanga
- D: Oddjob

42

Which British athlete married and divorced the swimmer and TV personality Sharron Davies?

- A: Colin Jackson
- B: Kriss Akabusi
- C: Roger Black
- D: Derek Redmond

43

What caused the equestrian events of the 1956 Melbourne Olympics to be held in Stockholm?

- A: Too hot for the horses
- B: Australia's quarantine laws
- C: Too expensive to transport the horses
- D: Inadequate stabling in Melbourne

44

In which sport might a McEgg or a McTwist be performed?

- A: Trampolining
- B: Synchronised swimming
- C: Snowboarding
- D: Pole vaulting

45

How many tiles are there in a mah-jong set?

- A: 100
- B: 122
- C: 130
- D: 144

50:50 Go to page 250　　Go to page 262　　? Answers on page 269

11 ◆ £64,000

46

Which herb is sometimes ungraciously called bastard fennel?

A: Dill

B: Chive

C: Sage

D: Thyme

47

Carom is a form of which of these sports?

A: Bowls

B: Billiards

C: Basketball

D: Baseball

48

In which of these rowing events has Steve Redgrave not won an Olympic gold medal?

A: Coxless four

B: Coxless pair

C: Double sculls

D: Coxed four

15 **£1 MILLION**

14 £500,000

13 £250,000

12 ◆ £125,000

11 ◆ £64,000

10 ◆ £32,000

9 ◆ £16,000

8 ◆ £8,000

7 ◆ £4,000

6 ◆ £2,000

5 ◆ £1,000

4 ◆ £500

3 ◆ £300

2 ◆ £200

1 ◆ £100

1

'Agaric' is an old term for any sort of what?

- A: Mushroom
- B: Tonic
- C: Cereal
- D: Herb

2

What was the middle name of the famous cricketer W G Grace?

- A: George
- B: Graham
- C: Godfrey
- D: Gilbert

3

Which equation indicates how much power is needed to operate an electrical appliance?

- A: Amps divided by volts
- B: Volts multiplied by watts
- C: Amps multiplied by volts
- D: Watts divided by volts

4

In 1989, what was surprising about Glasgow Rangers signing Maurice Johnston from the French club Nantes?

- A: 1st Roman Catholic to sign for the club
- B: 1st transfer from France to Scotland
- C: 1st £5 million transfer fee
- D: He was 39 years old at the time

5

What name is given to the part of a bell-rope prepared with inwoven wool for holding?

- A: Mary
- B: Sally
- C: Maggie
- D: Nelly

50:50 Go to page 250 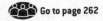 Go to page 262  Answers on page 269

12 ◆ £125,000

6

In which event did Ben Ainslie win an Olympic gold for Great Britain at the 2000 Sydney Games?

- A: Shooting
- B: Cycling
- C: Sailing
- D: Rowing

7

What is the main ingredient of passata?

- A: Potato
- B: Plum
- C: Tomato
- D: Carrot

8

The name of which game is derived from a derogatory term for a new recruit at the Woolwich Military Academy?

- A: Bandy
- B: Korfball
- C: Kabaddi
- D: Snooker

9

At what age can a person legally pilot a glider in the UK?

- A: 16
- B: 18
- C: 20
- D: 21

10

In which sport do competitors perform a 'telemark' landing?

- A: Ski jumping
- B: Gymnastics
- C: Parachuting
- D: Springboard diving

50:50 Go to page 250   Go to page 262   ? Answers on page 269

12 ◆ £125,000

11

Which female sprinter was given
the nicknamed 'La Gazelle'?

- A: Merlene Ottey
- B: Gail Devers
- C: Marie-Jose Perec
- D: Florence Griffith-Joyner

12

What does it mean if a plant is
described as being 'remontant'?

- A: Non-flowering
- B: Flowers more than once a season
- C: Climbing
- D: Spreading habit

13

What is the official distance
over which a drag race is timed?

- A: 110 yds
- B: 220 yds
- C: 440 yds
- D: 880 yds

14

In Indian cooking, what are gulab jamun?

- A: Curried lentils
- B: Fried dough balls
- C: Vegetable samosas
- D: Chicken pancakes

15

Which of horse racing's Classics is the oldest?

- A: Oaks
- B: Derby
- C: 2,000 Guineas
- D: St Leger

50:50 Go to page 251   Go to page 263   **?** Answers on page 269

12 ◆ £125,000

16

In which of the following countries would you find the Formula One racing track called the A1-Ring?

- A: Austria
- B: Hungary
- C: Germany
- D: Belgium

17

During which of the following activities would you be likely to use a 'coffee-grinder'?

- A: Windsailing
- B: Surfing
- C: Canoeing
- D: Yachting

18

Which other Argentinian footballer joined Tottenham Hotspur with Ossie Ardiles in 1978?

page 207

- A: Mario Kempes
- B: Ricardo Villa
- C: Nestor Benitez
- D: Antonio Rattin

19

What is the gyoji in Sumo wrestling?

- A: Belt
- B: Referee
- C: Ring
- D: Prize money

20

Which county is the main bacon producing area of Britain?

- A: Suffolk
- B: Essex
- C: Wiltshire
- D: Oxfordshire

50:50 Go to page 251   Go to page 263   ? Answers on page 269

12 ◆ £125,000

21

Which football club was stripped of the title after winning the 1993 European Cup Final?

A: AC Milan
B: Marseilles
C: Red Star Belgrade
D: Ajax

22

Where would you find a parc ferme?

A: Boules pitch
B: Running track
C: Ice hockey rink
D: Motor racing circuit

23

In which of the following was Barry Bucknell one of TV's original experts in the 1950s and 60s?

A: Magic
B: Gardening
C: Cookery
D: DIY

24

Which football league club are known as 'The Shaymen'?

A: Halifax Town
B: Stoke City
C: Leyton Orient
D: Preston North End

25

In March 2002, which cricketer set a record for the fastest test double century, taking just 153 deliveries?

A: Graham Thorpe
B: Steve Waugh
C: Ricky Ponting
D: Nathan Astle

 50:50 Go to page 251   Go to page 263   ? Answers on page 269

12 ◆ £125,000

26

What name is shared by a wild horse of western North America and the WWII US fighter plane designated the P-51?

- **A: Bronco**
- **B: Mustang**
- **C: Appaloosa**
- **D: Stallion**

27

Which skater was allowed to compete in the 1994 Winter Olympics despite being implicated in an attack on one of her rivals?

- **A: Nancy Kerrigan**
- **B: Tonya Harding**
- **C: Katarina Witt**
- **D: Tara Lipinski**

28

Who became the first Englishman to win the world rally title in 2001?

page 209

- **A: Colin McRae**
- **B: Richard Burns**
- **C: Andy Bull**
- **D: David Senior**

29

A familiar sight on racecourses in the 1950s, who or what was Prince Monolulu?

- **A: Jockey**
- **B: Trainer**
- **C: Owner**
- **D: Tipster**

30

Which sport returned to full medal status at the 1988 Olympics after an absence of over half a century?

- **A: Tug of War**
- **B: Football**
- **C: Tennis**
- **D: Polo**

50:50 Go to page 251 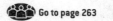 Go to page 263 **?** Answers on page 269

12 ◆ £125,000

31

If you ordered 'ostriche' in an Italian restaurant, what would you be served?

- A: Oysters
- B: Mussels
- C: Ostrich
- D: Duck

32

Which course hosted the Open Golf Championship for eleven consecutive years?

- A: St Andrews
- B: Prestwick
- C: Muirfield
- D: Troon

33

From which field event did record-breaking Cuban athlete Javier Sotomayor announce his retirement in 2001?

- A: Pole vault
- B: Long jump
- C: High jump
- D: Javelin

34

In winemaking, what name is given to the process in the Champagne method, of removing sediment from the bottle?

- A: Remuage
- B: Fining
- C: Degorgement
- D: Maceration

35

Which long standing British rod-caught fishing record was set by Georgina Ballantine in 1922?

- A: Heaviest salmon
- B: Heaviest trout
- C: Heaviest carp
- D: Longest eel

50:50 Go to page 251 Go to page 263 Answers on page 269

36

What name is given to a racehorse which represents the biggest liability to a bookmaker?

A: Bandit
B: Bogey
C: Banker
D: Bumper

37

In which sport in England has the premier knockout cup competition been sponsored by John Player Special, Pilkington, Tetley's Bitter and Powergen?

A: Cricket
B: Rugby League
C: Hockey
D: Rugby Union

38

What is the maximum score in a game of tenpin bowling?

A: 12
B: 300
C: 240
D: 100

39

At which British horse racing venue is the Rowley Mile a feature?

A: Aintree
B: Newmarket
C: Sandown Park
D: Goodwood

40

Which of the following is not a fragrance by Calvin Klein?

A: Escape
B: Contradiction
C: Freedom
D: Eternity

 50:50 Go to page 251   Go to page 263    ? Answers on page 269

12 ◆ £125,000

41

Which British university plays its
home cricket matches at Fenners?

A: Cambridge

B: Bristol

C: Nottingham

D: Oxford

42

The name of which Indian dish is derived from
a spicy stew brought to India by the Portuguese?

A: Korma

B: Balti

C: Vindaloo

D: Tikka

43

Which of these comic strip characters
appeared regularly in the Daily Express?

A: Fred Bassett

B: Rupert the Bear

C: Andy Capp

D: Garth

44

On which Caribbean island was West
Indies test cricketer Viv Richards born?

A: Barbados

B: Jamaica

C: Antigua

D: Grenada

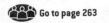 50:50 Go to page 251   Go to page 263   ? Answers on page 269

15		**£1 MILLION**
14		£500,000
13	◆	**£250,000**
12	◆	£125,000
11	◆	£64,000
10	◆	£32,000
9	◆	£16,000
8	◆	£8,000
7	◆	£4,000
6	◆	£2,000
5	◆	£1,000
4	◆	£500
3	◆	£300
2	◆	£200
1	◆	£100

13 ◆ £250,000

1

At which Grand Prix did Damon Hill win his first Formula One race?

- A: Hungarian
- B: Spanish
- C: British
- D: German

2

In which city is the John Innes Horticultural Institute based?

- A: Cambridge
- B: Norwich
- C: Chester
- D: Cardiff

3

In target shooting, what name is given to the area between the inner and outer rings?

- A: Magpie
- B: Rook
- C: Chough
- D: Jay

4

In which year did the England men's hockey team win an Olympic gold medal, when they defeated West Germany 3-1 in the final?

- A: 1984
- B: 1980
- C: 1988
- D: 1992

5

Athletes from which former nation were allowed to compete as 'independent Olympic participants' in 1992?

- A: Czechoslovakia
- B: USSR
- C: East Germany
- D: Yugoslavia

 50:50 Go to page 251　 Go to page 263　❓ Answers on page 269

13 ◆ £250,000

6

Which of these West Indian cricketers became Minister of Sport and Tourism for Barbados?

◆A: Wes Hall
◆B: Lance Gibbs
◆C: Rohan Kanhai
◆D: Clive Lloyd

7

Whom did Sonny Liston beat to win the world heavyweight boxing championship in 1962?

◆A: Ingemar Johannson
◆B: Floyd Patterson
◆C: Cassius Clay
◆D: Rocky Marciano

8

Which of the following was named European Car of the Year 2002?

◆A: Alfa Romeo 147
◆B: Renault Laguna
◆C: Fiat Stilo
◆D: Peugeot 307

9

What colour dot indicates the slowest ball in a game of squash?

◆A: White
◆B: Red
◆C: Blue
◆D: Yellow

10

Which of the following is a type of artists' drawing paper?

◆A: Delacroix
◆B: Ingres
◆C: Poussin
◆D: Rubens

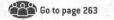 50:50 Go to page 251   Go to page 263    ? Answers on page 269

13 ◆ £250,000

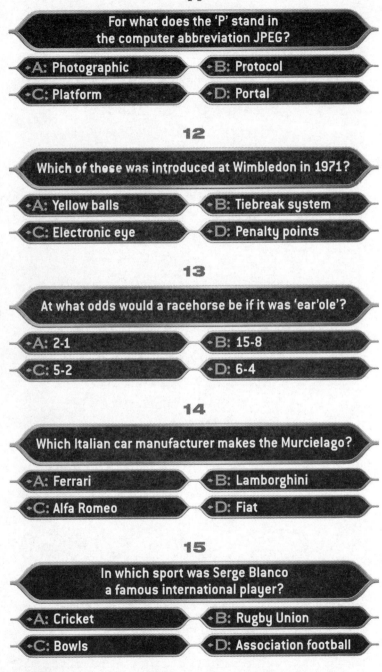

11

For what does the 'P' stand in
the computer abbreviation JPEG?

A: Photographic | B: Protocol
C: Platform | D: Portal

12

Which of those was introduced at Wimbledon in 1971?

A: Yellow balls | B: Tiebreak system
C: Electronic eye | D: Penalty points

13

At what odds would a racehorse be if it was 'ear'ole'?

A: 2-1 | B: 15-8
C: 5-2 | D: 6-4

14

Which Italian car manufacturer makes the Murcielago?

A: Ferrari | B: Lamborghini
C: Alfa Romeo | D: Fiat

15

In which sport was Serge Blanco
a famous international player?

A: Cricket | B: Rugby Union
C: Bowls | D: Association football

50:50 Go to page 251   Go to page 263   Answers on page 269

13 ◆ £250,000

16

Whom did Virginia Wade defeat in the final of the 1977 Wimbledon Ladies Singles?

- A: Chris Evert
- B: Betty Stove
- C: Margaret Court
- D: Billie Jean King

17

Which of these sailing trophies was renamed the Volvo Ocean Race in 2001?

- A: Vendée Globe
- B: America's Cup
- C: Whitbread Round-the-World-Race
- D: Jules Verne Trophy

18

Which show jumping event tests a horse's ability to jump a decreasing number of obstacles, the height of which increases throughout the competition?

- A: Bareme
- B: Piaffe
- C: Volte
- D: Puissance

19

What amp fuse should you use for a hairdryer with a 700 watt power rating?

- A: 5 amp
- B: 13 amp
- C: 3 amp
- D: 7 amp

20

In which of these sports might a player execute a 'bunt'?

- A: Baseball
- B: Badminton
- C: Volleyball
- D: Basketball

 50:50 Go to page 251   Go to page 263   ? Answers on page 269

13 ◆ £250,000

21

Which of these boxers won world
titles in five different weight classes?

- A: Jake LaMotta
- B: Marvin Hagler
- C: Sugar Ray Leonard
- D: Sugar Ray Robinson

22

What colour is produced by the addition
of cobalt carbonate to a pottery glaze?

- A: Red
- B: White
- C: Brown
- D: Blue

23

Which high street fashion retailer was founded in 1916 by
Sam Farmer - its name coming from a variety of rambling rose?

- A: Monsoon
- B: Dorothy Perkins
- C: Laura Ashley
- D: Bon Marché

24

In which sport in South Africa
is the Currie Cup competed for?

- A: Tennis
- B: Cricket
- C: Rugby Union
- D: Golf

25

Trina Gulliver was the 2001 and 2002 women's
world champion at which of the following?

- A: Badminton
- B: Darts
- C: Bowls
- D: Speed skating

50:50 Go to page 251   Go to page 263   Answers on page 269

13 ◆ £250,000

26

Which was the first country to win football's World Cup outside their own continent?

- A: Italy
- B: Brazil
- C: Argentina
- D: West Germany

27

In which sport is the Iditarod Trail raced annually?

- A: Motor rallying
- B: Cyclo cross
- C: Dog sled racing
- D: Nordic skiing

28

The West Indies cricket legend Malcolm Marshall played for which of these English counties?

- A: Lancashire
- B: Yorkshire
- C: Worcestershire
- D: Hampshire

29

Which sport was invented in Holyoke, Massachusetts in the 1890s by William Morgan?

- A: Basketball
- B: Ice hockey
- C: Baseball
- D: Volleyball

30

Which British former world boxing champion was nicknamed the 'Paddington Express'?

- A: Terry Downes
- B: Alan Minter
- C: Terry Marsh
- D: Freddie Mills

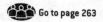 50:50 Go to page 251   Go to page 263    ? Answers on page 269

31

In the ancient game of Knur and Spell, what is the 'Knur'?

- A: Bat
- B: Ball
- C: Player
- D: Target

32

In genealogical terms, which word means a widow who has not married again?

- A: Relicta
- B: Vidua
- C: Testatrix
- D: Virgo

33

Who, in 1993, became the first black footballer to captain England in a full international?

- A: Viv Anderson
- B: Les Ferdinand
- C: Des Walker
- D: Paul Ince

34

Which sport has a scoring area called a 'house', which is 12 feet in diameter?

- A: Curling
- B: Archery
- C: Clay pigeon shooting
- D: Target golf

35

Who was the first tennis player to win the US Open on three different surfaces?

- A: John McEnroe
- B: Björn Borg
- C: Jimmy Connors
- D: Boris Becker

50:50 Go to page 251   Go to page 263   Answers on page 269

13 ◆ £250,000

36

Which of the following games is thought to have originated in the Basque regions of France and Spain?

- A: Pato
- B: Boules
- C: Pétanque
- D: Pelota

37

Opened in 1993, in which country is the Olympic Museum?

- A: Switzerland
- B: Greece
- C: USA
- D: France

38

Which was the world's first purpose-built motor racing circuit?

- A: Monza
- B: Brooklands
- C: Le Mans
- D: Brands Hatch

39

What type of painters were known as 'limners'?

- A: Landscapists
- B: Watercolourists
- C: Muralists
- D: Miniaturists

40

Which of these is the technical name for a cat's whiskers?

- A: Papillae
- B: Fibrillae
- C: Vibrissae
- D: Quillidae

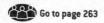 50:50 Go to page 251    Go to page 263   ? Answers on page 269

15		£1 MILLION
14	◆	**£500,000**
13	◆	£250,000
12	◆	£125,000
11	◆	£64,000
10	◆	£32,000
9	◆	£16,000
8	◆	£8,000
7	◆	£4,000
6	◆	£2,000
5	◆	£1,000
4	◆	£500
3	◆	£300
2	◆	£200
1	◆	£100

1

In January 2002, which football club offered to share its ground with York City?

A: Rotherham United

B: Hull City

C: Chesterfield

D: Bradford City

2

In March 2002, which England cricketer scored his maiden test century in the first Test against New Zealand?

A: Graham Thorpe

B: Paul Foster

C: Andrew Flintoff

D: Mark Ramprakash

3

In which field was Robert Harbin a famous TV performer in the 1950s?

A: Magic

B: Cookery

C: DIY

D: Gardening

4

Which of the following is a type of fence in show jumping?

A: Devil's Punchbowl

B: Hog's Back

C: Snake Pass

D: Cheddar Gorge

5

What was the name of Britain's first department store which opened in 1863, using the slogan 'One-stop Shop'?

A: Bentalls

B: Selfridge's

C: Whiteleys

D: Marshall and Snelgrove

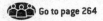 **50:50** Go to page 252   Go to page 264   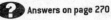 **?** Answers on page 270

14 ◆ £500,000

6

What is the first name of the Brazilian footballer whose other names are Luiz Nazario da Lima?

- A: Ronaldo
- B: Rivaldo
- C: Denilson
- D: Pele

7

In which Italian city did the Bellini cocktail originate?

- A: Rome
- B: Florence
- C: Venice
- D: Milan

8

What name is given to the dips on a roulette wheel into which the ball falls?

page
225

- A: Rafts
- B: Canoes
- C: Smacks
- D: Floats

9

In which women's championship is the winner presented with the Venus Rosewater dish?

- A: Open golf
- B: World figure skating
- C: Wimbledon singles
- D: World Open squash

10

Who would be most likely to perform prestidigitation?

- A: Magician
- B: Boxer
- C: Wine taster
- D: Clairvoyant

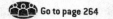 

50:50 Go to page 252   Go to page 264   ? Answers on page 270

11

Which of these Olympic sports was last seen in the 1920 Antwerp Games?

A: Golf

B: Motor boating

C: Tug of war

D: Cricket

12

What is the length of a standard roll of British wallpaper?

A: 20 metres

B: 15 metres

C: 10.5 metres

D: 20.5 metres

13

In which sport is the 'Ram muay' ritual performed before the start of a contest?

A: Sumo wrestling

B: Thai kick boxing

C: Kendo

D: Judo

14

As of 2002, who scored the fastest goal in the English FA Cup final, timed at just 43 seconds?

A: Clive Allen

B: Ian Rush

C: Roberto di Matteo

D: Patrick Vieira

15

In which Olympic sport is a Keirin event contested?

A: Equestrian

B: Fencing

C: Cycling

D: Canoeing

 50:50 Go to page 252   Go to page 264   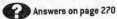 ? Answers on page 270

14 ◆ £500,000

16

Which former tennis champion was nicknamed 'the Bounding Basque'?

A: René Lacoste

B: Pancho Gonzales

C: Jean Borotra

D: Jaroslav Drobny

17

To which species of flower does the Jerusalem artichoke belong?

A: Sunflower

B: Dahlia

C: Chrysanthemum

D: Iris

18

In which sport is the Henri Delaunay cup a major international competition?

page **227**

A: Association football

B: Yachting

C: Rowing

D: Rugby Union

19

In 1999, which football ground hosted the last European Cup Winners' Cup Final?

A: Old Trafford

B: Villa Park

C: Wembley

D: St James' Park

20

What, in Germany, is an 'abfahrt'?

A: Motorway

B: Town hall

C: Downhill ski run

D: Escalator

50:50 Go to page 252    Go to page 264   ❓ Answers on page 270

14 ◆ £500,000

21

Which horse won the 2002 Epsom Derby?

- A: Hawk Wing
- B: Moon Ballad
- C: Kournakova
- D: High Chaparral

22

What form of transport is used in the annual 'Race Across America'?

- A: Bicycle
- B: Motor car
- C: Horse
- D: Motorcycle

23

In which Scottish administrative region is the famous Muirfield golf course?

- A: Falkirk
- B: East Lothian
- C: Moray
- D: Inverclyde

24

What is the former Wimbledon champion Virginia Wade's real first name?

- A: Sally
- B: Susan
- C: Samantha
- D: Sarah

25

Which of these is not a suit in a standard game of Mah-Jong?

- A: Flowers
- B: Bamboo
- C: Circles
- D: Characters

 50:50 Go to page 252　　Go to page 264　　 **?** Answers on page 270

26

For which county did former England captain Brian Close play first class cricket after he left Yorkshire?

- A: Lancashire
- B: Gloucestershire
- C: Surrey
- D: Somerset

27

The Wooden Spoon Society is a major charity connected with which of these sports?

- A: Athletics
- B: Cricket
- C: Boxing
- D: Rugby Union

28

Petroselinum crispum is the Latin name for which popular herb?

page
229

- A: Parsley
- B: Chervil
- C: Tarragon
- D: Mint

29

In 2002, which horse failed in its attempt to win the Cheltenham Gold Cup for a record fourth time?

- A: Hors La Roi
- B: Marble Arch
- C: Istabraq
- D: Seebald

30

Which writer is credited with the first written reference to a Punch and Judy show in England?

- A: Samuel Pepys
- B: Samuel Johnson
- C: Charles Dickens
- D: Thomas Hardy

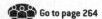

31

In which of these games is the Venice Cup a major competition for women?

A: Chess

B: Bridge

C: Whist

D: Backgammon

32

In which county is the Pendon Museum of Miniature Landscape and Transport?

A: Lancashire

B: Oxfordshire

C: Derbyshire

D: Devon

33

What nickname was given to the Celtic football team that won the European Cup in 1967?

A: Turin Tigers

B: Warsaw Wolves

C: Lisbon Lions

D: Rotterdam Rams

34

In which Olympic sport was a Jamaican team featured in the film 'Cool Runnings'?

A: Ski jump

B: Marathon

C: 4 x 100m relay

D: Bobsleigh

35

In a standard pack of playing cards, which face card is sometimes known as the 'suicide king'?

A: King of Spades

B: King of Hearts

C: King of Clubs

D: King of Diamonds

50:50 Go to page 252 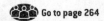 Go to page 264 ? Answers on page 270

36

Which of these British darts players is nicknamed 'The Count'?

A: John Walton

B: Ted Hankey

C: Colin Monk

D: Mervyn King

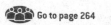 50:50 Go to page 252　Go to page 264　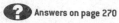 Answers on page 270

15 ◆ £1 MILLION

14 ◆ £500,000

13 ◆ £250,000

12 ◆ £125,000

11 ◆ £64,000

10 ◆ £32,000

9 ◆ £16,000

8 ◆ £8,000

7 ◆ £4,000

6 ◆ £2,000

5 ◆ £1,000

4 ◆ £500

3 ◆ £300

2 ◆ £200

1 ◆ £100

15 ◆ £1,000,000

1

Which former Wimbledon Men's Singles champion's middle name is Rune?

- A: Boris Becker
- B: Björn Borg
- C: Pat Cash
- D: Andre Agassi

2

What, in Austrian cuisine, are 'nockerln'?

- A: Sweets
- B: Potatoes
- C: Dumplings
- D: Glacé fruits

3

What name connects the winning horse and the race sponsors of the 1991 Aintree Grand National?

- A: Martell
- B: Seagram
- C: Ever Ready
- D: Duracell

4

Which of these tourist attractions was designed and created by Gutzon Borglum?

- A: Mount Rushmore
- B: Yellowstone National Park
- C: Disneyland
- D: Empire State Building

5

In which of these events is the women's world record a greater distance than the men's?

- A: Hammer
- B: Javelin
- C: Shot Put
- D: Discus

 50:50 Go to page 252   Go to page 264   ? Answers on page 270

15 ◆ £1,000,000

6

Which of these liqueurs is not orange flavoured?

A: Cointreau

B: Curaçao

C: Galliano

D: Grand Marnier

7

In harness racing, what term is applied to a horse that moves both front and hind legs on the same side at the same time?

A: Trotter

B: Prancer

C: Standard

D: Pacer

8

Which of these moves in judo is a hip throw?

A: Kata-ha-jime

B: O-soto-gari

C: Ne-waza

D: O-goshi

9

Who was the first boxer to win the World Heavyweight title wearing gloves under the Queensberry Rules?

A: John L Sullivan

B: James J Corbett

C: James J Jeffries

D: Jack Johnson

10

Which ex-Leeds United player has not been manager of the club?

A: Allan Clarke

B: Terry Cooper

C: Billy Bremner

D: Eddie Gray

50:50 Go to page 252   Go to page 264   ? Answers on page 270

15 ◆ £1,000,000

11

What nickname was given to Japan's famous former champion sumo wrestler Konishiki on account of his size?

◆A: Fatbelly   ◆B: Brick wall

◆C: Dump truck   ◆D: Bulldozer

12

Traditionally avgolemono, a soup or sauce made of eggs, lemon juice, and rice comes from which country?

◆A: Italy   ◆B: Greece

◆C: Spain   ◆D: Romania

13

In which sport did Janet Altwegg win an Olympic gold medal for Britain in 1952?

◆A: Skating   ◆B: Skiing

◆C: Luge   ◆D: Bobsleigh

14

The ancient Central American game of 'pok-tapok' was a forerunner of which modern day sport?

◆A: Pelota   ◆B: Basketball

◆C: Golf   ◆D: Tennis

15

Which famous annual British sporting event first took place in 1829?

◆A: University Boat Race   ◆B: Aintree Grand National

◆C: Horse of the Year Show ◆D: Wimbledon Championships

50:50 Go to page 252   Go to page 264   ? Answers on page 270

15 ◆ £1,000,000

16

Which footballer holds the record for the most goals scored during a World Cup tournament?

- A: Pelé
- B: Sàndor Kocsis
- C: Gerd Müller
- D: Just Fontaine

17

Which sport has variations called Glima in Iceland, Kushti in India and Yagli in Turkey?

- A: Polo
- B: Wrestling
- C: Weightlifting
- D: Golf

18

What was the full first name of the American photographer, painter and film-maker Man Ray?

- A: Manfred
- B: Mansfield
- C: Emanuel
- D: Manuel

19

Which was the only sport for women at the first British Empire Games in 1930?

- A: Bowls
- B: Tennis
- C: Show jumping
- D: Swimming

20

Dr Spock, famous for his book on baby care, won a gold medal at the 1924 Olympics – in which sport?

- A: Swimming
- B: Rowing
- C: Fencing
- D: Athletics

 50:50 Go to page 252    Go to page 264   ? Answers on page 270

15 ◆ £1,000,000

21

In which of these water sports
might a 'goofy-footer' participate?

A: Water skiing

B: Yachting

C: Synchronized swimming

D: Surfing

22

Which US city is the home of the Griffith Park Zoo?

A: Houston

B: Los Angeles

C: Cleveland

D: Seattle

23

The name of Sunderland FC's home ground is the
same as the home ground of which Portuguese club?

A: Porto

B: Benfica

C: Boavista

D: Sporting Lisbon

24

Which British footballer once remarked of his
time in Italy, 'it was like living in a foreign country'?

A: Paul Gascoigne

B: Ray Wilkins

C: Ian Rush

D: David Platt

25

A 'patzer' is a poor player at which game?

A: Bridge

B: Canasta

C: Chess

D: Backgammon

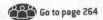 50:50 Go to page 252  Go to page 264 ? Answers on page 270

15 ◆ £1,000,000

26

Which North American ski resort
is often called the 'island in the sky'?

◆A: Snowshoe ◆B: Sugarbush

◆C: Sugar Bowl ◆D: Snowbasin

27

What was the real first name of the
legendary baseball star Babe Ruth?

◆A: Thomas ◆B: Charles

◆C: George ◆D: Benjamin

28

Which of these cricketer's fathers
did not also play test cricket for England?

◆A: Mark Butcher ◆B: Chris Cowdrey

◆C: Richard Illingworth ◆D: Alec Stewart

29

By what biblical name is the plant
olibanum sometimes known?

◆A: Myrrh ◆B: Burning bush

◆C: Frankincense ◆D: Manna

30

Which perfume house launched
the fragrance 'Pleasures' in 1996?

◆A: Yves St Laurent ◆B: Lancôme

◆C: Estée Lauder ◆D: Nina Ricci

 50:50 Go to page 252 Go to page 264 ? Answers on page 270

15 ◆ £1,000,000

31

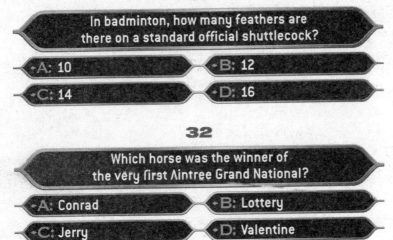

In badminton, how many feathers are
there on a standard official shuttlecock?

◆A: 10 ◆B: 12

◆C: 14 ◆D: 16

32

Which horse was the winner of
the very first Aintree Grand National?

◆A: Conrad ◆B: Lottery

◆C: Jerry ◆D: Valentine

50:50 Go to page 252   Go to page 264   **?** Answers on page 270

50:50

£100

1	Options remaining are A and B	38	Options remaining are A and D
2	Options remaining are A and D	39	Options remaining are C and D
3	Options remaining are B and C	40	Options remaining are A and C
4	Options remaining are B and C	41	Options remaining are A and C
5	Options remaining are A and B	42	Options remaining are B and D
6	Options remaining are C and D	43	Options remaining are A and C
7	Options remaining are B and D	44	Options remaining are A and D
8	Options remaining are A and B	45	Options remaining are B and D
9	Options remaining are A and B	46	Options remaining are B and C
10	Options remaining are B and D	47	Options remaining are C and D
11	Options remaining are A and B	48	Options remaining are B and C
12	Options remaining are C and D	49	Options remaining are C and D
13	Options remaining are A and D	50	Options remaining are A and D
14	Options remaining are A and B	51	Options remaining are A and B
15	Options remaining are A and C	52	Options remaining are B and C
16	Options remaining are A and D	53	Options remaining are B and C
17	Options remaining are B and C	54	Options remaining are B and C
18	Options remaining are B and C	55	Options remaining are B and D
19	Options remaining are B and D	56	Options remaining are A and C
20	Options remaining are B and C	57	Options remaining are C and D
21	Options remaining are A and D	58	Options remaining are A and D
22	Options remaining are A and B	59	Options remaining are C and D
23	Options remaining are A and D	60	Options remaining are B and C
24	Options remaining are A and B	61	Options remaining are A and B
25	Options remaining are B and D	62	Options remaining are A and C
26	Options remaining are C and D	63	Options remaining are A and D
27	Options remaining are A and B	64	Options remaining are C and D
28	Options remaining are A and C	65	Options remaining are A and C
29	Options remaining are B and C	66	Options remaining are C and D
30	Options remaining are A and D	67	Options remaining are A and B
31	Options remaining are A and B	68	Options remaining are A and C
32	Options remaining are A and C	69	Options remaining are B and D
33	Options remaining are B and D	70	Options remaining are B and C
34	Options remaining are A and B	71	Options remaining are A and C
35	Options remaining are B and C	72	Options remaining are A and C
36	Options remaining are C and D	73	Options remaining are A and C
37	Options remaining are A and D	74	Options remaining are C and D

50:50

75 Options remaining are A and B
76 Options remaining are C and D
77 Options remaining are B and D
78 Options remaining are A and B
79 Options remaining are B and D
80 Options remaining are A and D
81 Options remaining are A and B

82 Options remaining are A and C
83 Options remaining are A and C
84 Options remaining are A and C
85 Options remaining are B and D
86 Options remaining are A and D
87 Options remaining are A and B
88 Options remaining are C and D

£200

1 Options remaining are B and C
2 Options remaining are B and C
3 Options remaining are B and D
4 Options remaining are A and D
5 Options remaining are B and C
6 Options remaining are B and D
7 Options remaining are B and D
8 Options remaining are B and D
9 Options remaining are B and D
10 Options remaining are C and D
11 Options remaining are B and D
12 Options remaining are B and D
13 Options remaining are A and C
14 Options remaining are A and C
15 Options remaining are A and B
16 Options remaining are B and D
17 Options remaining are B and D
18 Options remaining are A and B
19 Options remaining are A and C
20 Options remaining are B and D
21 Options remaining are B and C
22 Options remaining are A and C
23 Options remaining are B and D
24 Options remaining are A and B
25 Options remaining are B and D
26 Options remaining are B and C
27 Options remaining are B and C
28 Options remaining are B and C
29 Options remaining are C and D
30 Options remaining are B and D
31 Options remaining are A and D
32 Options remaining are B and C

33 Options remaining are B and C
34 Options remaining are A and B
35 Options remaining are A and B
36 Options remaining are B and D
37 Options remaining are B and D
38 Options remaining are B and C
39 Options remaining are A and B
40 Options remaining are A and C
41 Options remaining are A and B
42 Options remaining are A and B
43 Options remaining are A and D
44 Options remaining are C and D
45 Options remaining are B and C
46 Options remaining are A and B
47 Options remaining are A and D
48 Options remaining are B and C
49 Options remaining are B and D
50 Options remaining are B and D
51 Options remaining are A and C
52 Options remaining are C and D
53 Options remaining are B and C
54 Options remaining are A and D
55 Options remaining are B and D
56 Options remaining are B and C
57 Options remaining are C and D
58 Options remaining are B and C
59 Options remaining are A and B
60 Options remaining are B and C
61 Options remaining are C and D
62 Options remaining are C and D
63 Options remaining are C and D
64 Options remaining are B and D

50:50

65	Options remaining are A and C	75	Options remaining are B and D
66	Options remaining are A and B	76	Options remaining are B and C
67	Options remaining are A and C	77	Options remaining are B and D
68	Options remaining are B and C	78	Options remaining are B and D
69	Options remaining are B and D	79	Options remaining are B and C
70	Options remaining are A and B	80	Options remaining are A and D
71	Options remaining are A and B	81	Options remaining are A and C
72	Options remaining are B and C	82	Options remaining are A and C
73	Options remaining are B and D	83	Options remaining are A and C
74	Options remaining are B and C	84	Options remaining are B and C

£300

1	Options remaining are A and C	30	Options remaining are A and D
2	Options remaining are A and B	31	Options remaining are C and D
3	Options remaining are A and D	32	Options remaining are A and B
4	Options remaining are C and D	33	Options remaining are A and B
5	Options remaining are C and D	34	Options remaining are A and C
6	Options remaining are A and D	35	Options remaining are A and D
7	Options remaining are A and B	36	Options remaining are B and C
8	Options remaining are A and C	37	Options remaining are A and D
9	Options remaining are B and C	38	Options remaining are A and B
10	Options remaining are A and B	39	Options remaining are B and C
11	Options remaining are A and D	40	Options remaining are B and C
12	Options remaining are A and C	41	Options remaining are B and C
13	Options remaining are A and C	42	Options remaining are A and C
14	Options remaining are A and C	43	Options remaining are A and C
15	Options remaining are B and C	44	Options remaining are A and C
16	Options remaining are A and C	45	Options remaining are A and B
17	Options remaining are B and D	46	Options remaining are B and C
18	Options remaining are A and B	47	Options remaining are B and D
19	Options remaining are A and B	48	Options remaining are A and B
20	Options remaining are A and B	49	Options remaining are A and B
21	Options remaining are A and C	50	Options remaining are B and C
22	Options remaining are A and B	51	Options remaining are A and C
23	Options remaining are C and D	52	Options remaining are B and C
24	Options remaining are A and D	53	Options remaining are A and C
25	Options remaining are A and C	54	Options remaining are C and D
26	Options remaining are A and C	55	Options remaining are C and D
27	Options remaining are A and B	56	Options remaining are C and D
28	Options remaining are A and C	57	Options remaining are A and B
29	Options remaining are A and B	58	Options remaining are C and D

50:50

59	Options remaining are A and D	70	Options remaining are A and B
60	Options remaining are A and D	71	Options remaining are B and C
61	Options remaining are B and D	72	Options remaining are B and C
62	Options remaining are C and D	73	Options remaining are B and C
63	Options remaining are A and D	74	Options remaining are A and D
64	Options remaining are A and B	75	Options remaining are A and B
65	Options remaining are A and D	76	Options remaining are A and D
66	Options remaining are C and D	77	Options remaining are C and D
67	Options remaining are B and D	78	Options remaining are A and B
68	Options remaining are A and C	79	Options remaining are B and C
69	Options remaining are A and D	80	Options remaining are A and C

£500

1	Options remaining are A and B	29	Options remaining are A and C
2	Options remaining are B and C	30	Options remaining are C and D
3	Options remaining are A and B	31	Options remaining are A and C
4	Options remaining are A and C	32	Options remaining are A and B
5	Options remaining are A and B	33	Options remaining are A and C
6	Options remaining are B and D	34	Options remaining are A and C
7	Options remaining are A and D	35	Options remaining are C and D
8	Options remaining are B and D	36	Options remaining are B and D
9	Options remaining are A and C	37	Options remaining are A and B
10	Options remaining are C and D	38	Options remaining are A and C
11	Options remaining are A and B	39	Options remaining are B and D
12	Options remaining are A and B	40	Options remaining are A and D
13	Options remaining are A and B	41	Options remaining are B and C
14	Options remaining are A and B	42	Options remaining are B and C
15	Options remaining are A and C	43	Options remaining are C and D
16	Options remaining are C and D	44	Options remaining are A and D
17	Options remaining are A and B	45	Options remaining are A and C
18	Options remaining are A and D	46	Options remaining are B and D
19	Options remaining are B and C	47	Options remaining are B and C
20	Options remaining are B and D	48	Options remaining are A and B
21	Options remaining are C and D	49	Options remaining are A and D
22	Options remaining are C and D	50	Options remaining are A and D
23	Options remaining are A and B	51	Options remaining are A and C
24	Options remaining are A and B	52	Options remaining are B and C
25	Options remaining are B and C	53	Options remaining are B and C
26	Options remaining are C and D	54	Options remaining are A and D
27	Options remaining are A and B	55	Options remaining are A and C
28	Options remaining are A and C	56	Options remaining are B and C

50:50

57	Options remaining are C and D	67	Options remaining are B and D
58	Options remaining are B and C	68	Options remaining are B and D
59	Options remaining are A and D	69	Options remaining are A and C
60	Options remaining are B and D	70	Options remaining are A and B
61	Options remaining are B and C	71	Options remaining are B and C
62	Options remaining are B and D	72	Options remaining are A and D
63	Options remaining are C and D	73	Options remaining are A and B
64	Options remaining are C and D	74	Options remaining are A and B
65	Options remaining are B and C	75	Options remaining are C and D
66	Options remaining are C and D	76	Options remaining are A and B

£1,000

1	Options remaining are B and C	30	Options remaining are A and D
2	Options remaining are B and D	31	Options remaining are A and B
3	Options remaining are B and C	32	Options remaining are A and C
4	Options remaining are B and D	33	Options remaining are B and D
5	Options remaining are C and D	34	Options remaining are C and D
6	Options remaining are A and B	35	Options remaining are C and D
7	Options remaining are A and D	36	Options remaining are A and B
8	Options remaining are B and C	37	Options remaining are B and D
9	Options remaining are A and D	38	Options remaining are C and D
10	Options remaining are B and D	39	Options remaining are A and B
11	Options remaining are A and C	40	Options remaining are C and D
12	Options remaining are A and C	41	Options remaining are B and C
13	Options remaining are A and D	42	Options remaining are B and D
14	Options remaining are B and C	43	Options remaining are A and C
15	Options remaining are B and C	44	Options remaining are B and D
16	Options remaining are A and B	45	Options remaining are C and D
17	Options remaining are A and D	46	Options remaining are B and C
18	Options remaining are B and D	47	Options remaining are C and D
19	Options remaining are B and D	48	Options remaining are C and D
20	Options remaining are B and D	49	Options remaining are A and C
21	Options remaining are B and C	50	Options remaining are B and D
22	Options remaining are B and C	51	Options remaining are A and C
23	Options remaining are A and B	52	Options remaining are B and D
24	Options remaining are A and D	53	Options remaining are A and B
25	Options remaining are B and C	54	Options remaining are C and D
26	Options remaining are A and B	55	Options remaining are A and C
27	Options remaining are B and C	56	Options remaining are A and D
28	Options remaining are A and D	57	Options remaining are C and D
29	Options remaining are B and C	58	Options remaining are B and C

50:50

59	Options remaining are A and B	66	Options remaining are A and D
60	Options remaining are A and D	67	Options remaining are A and B
61	Options remaining are A and C	68	Options remaining are A and D
62	Options remaining are B and C	69	Options remaining are B and D
63	Options remaining are A and B	70	Options remaining are A and B
64	Options remaining are B and C	71	Options remaining are A and B
65	Options remaining are A and D	72	Options remaining are A and B

£2,000

1	Options remaining are A and B	32	Options remaining are A and B
2	Options remaining are B and D	33	Options remaining are A and D
3	Options remaining are B and C	34	Options remaining are A and D
4	Options remaining are B and D	35	Options remaining are A and B
5	Options remaining are C and D	36	Options remaining are B and C
6	Options remaining are B and C	37	Options remaining are C and D
7	Options remaining are B and C	38	Options remaining are A and D
8	Options remaining are A and C	39	Options remaining are A and D
9	Options remaining are A and C	40	Options remaining are B and D
10	Options remaining are B and D	41	Options remaining are A and C
11	Options remaining are B and C	42	Options remaining are A and D
12	Options remaining are A and D	43	Options remaining are A and D
13	Options remaining are B and D	44	Options remaining are A and B
14	Options remaining are A and C	45	Options remaining are A and B
15	Options remaining are B and C	46	Options remaining are B and C
16	Options remaining are A and B	47	Options remaining are C and D
17	Options remaining are A and B	48	Options remaining are A and D
18	Options remaining are B and C	49	Options remaining are B and D
19	Options remaining are B and D	50	Options remaining are B and D
20	Options remaining are A and C	51	Options remaining are A and C
21	Options remaining are A and B	52	Options remaining are B and D
22	Options remaining are B and D	53	Options remaining are A and B
23	Options remaining are B and C	54	Options remaining are C and D
24	Options remaining are A and B	55	Options remaining are A and D
25	Options remaining are B and C	56	Options remaining are A and C
26	Options remaining are B and D	57	Options remaining are B and C
27	Options remaining are A and D	58	Options remaining are C and D
28	Options remaining are A and D	59	Options remaining are A and D
29	Options remaining are A and C	60	Options remaining are C and D
30	Options remaining are A and B	61	Options remaining are B and D
31	Options remaining are A and C	62	Options remaining are B and D

50:50

£4,000

£8,000

1	Options remaining are B and C	31	Options remaining are C and D
2	Options remaining are B and D	32	Options remaining are A and B
3	Options remaining are B and C	33	Options remaining are C and D
4	Options remaining are C and D	34	Options remaining are B and C
5	Options remaining are A and B	35	Options remaining are A and C
6	Options remaining are B and D	36	Options remaining are B and C
7	Options remaining are A and C	37	Options remaining are A and D
8	Options remaining are A and B	38	Options remaining are A and C
9	Options remaining are B and D	39	Options remaining are A and C
10	Options remaining are B and C	40	Options remaining are A and D
11	Options remaining are A and B	41	Options remaining are A and D
12	Options remaining are B and D	42	Options remaining are A and D
13	Options remaining are B and D	43	Options remaining are B and C
14	Options remaining are B and D	44	Options remaining are A and D
15	Options remaining are B and C	45	Options remaining are A and B
16	Options remaining are A and B	46	Options remaining are A and C
17	Options remaining are B and C	47	Options remaining are A and D
18	Options remaining are A and C	48	Options remaining are B and C
19	Options remaining are A and B	49	Options remaining are A and D
20	Options remaining are C and D	50	Options remaining are B and C
21	Options remaining are A and C	51	Options remaining are A and B
22	Options remaining are A and C	52	Options remaining are A and C
23	Options remaining are A and D	53	Options remaining are B and D
24	Options remaining are A and C	54	Options remaining are B and C
25	Options remaining are A and C	55	Options remaining are B and D
26	Options remaining are B and D	56	Options remaining are A and B
27	Options remaining are C and D	57	Options remaining are B and D
28	Options remaining are A and C	58	Options remaining are A and D
29	Options remaining are A and C	59	Options remaining are A and D
30	Options remaining are A and D	60	Options remaining are A and B

£16,000

1	Options remaining are B and D	10	Options remaining are B and D
2	Options remaining are B and C	11	Options remaining are B and D
3	Options remaining are A and C	12	Options remaining are C and D
4	Options remaining are A and B	13	Options remaining are C and D
5	Options remaining are C and D	14	Options remaining are A and C
6	Options remaining are C and D	15	Options remaining are B and D
7	Options remaining are A and C	16	Options remaining are A and B
8	Options remaining are A and D	17	Options remaining are B and D
9	Options remaining are A and C	18	Options remaining are B and D

19 Options remaining are A and C	38 Options remaining are A and C
20 Options remaining are A and B	39 Options remaining are B and D
21 Options remaining are A and C	40 Options remaining are C and D
22 Options remaining are A and C	41 Options remaining are A and C
23 Options remaining are B and D	42 Options remaining are C and D
24 Options remaining are A and B	43 Options remaining are A and B
25 Options remaining are B and C	44 Options remaining are B and C
26 Options remaining are C and D	45 Options remaining are C and D
27 Options remaining are A and B	46 Options remaining are B and D
28 Options remaining are A and D	47 Options remaining are B and D
29 Options remaining are A and C	48 Options remaining are B and C
30 Options remaining are B and C	49 Options remaining are B and C
31 Options remaining are A and D	50 Options remaining are A and D
32 Options remaining are C and D	51 Options remaining are A and C
33 Options remaining are A and C	52 Options remaining are A and B
34 Options remaining are A and B	53 Options remaining are C and D
35 Options remaining are A and C	54 Options remaining are B and C
36 Options remaining are A and B	55 Options remaining are A and B
37 Options remaining are A and D	56 Options remaining are B and C

£32,000

1 Options remaining are A and B	21 Options remaining are C and D
2 Options remaining are A and B	22 Options remaining are C and D
3 Options remaining are A and B	23 Options remaining are A and C
4 Options remaining are B and D	24 Options remaining are A and C
5 Options remaining are A and D	25 Options remaining are A and B
6 Options remaining are A and D	26 Options remaining are B and D
7 Options remaining are C and D	27 Options remaining are B and D
8 Options remaining are C and D	28 Options remaining are C and D
9 Options remaining are A and C	29 Options remaining are B and C
10 Options remaining are A and B	30 Options remaining are B and C
11 Options remaining are A and C	31 Options remaining are C and D
12 Options remaining are A and C	32 Options remaining are A and D
13 Options remaining are A and C	33 Options remaining are A and B
14 Options remaining are B and C	34 Options remaining are B and D
15 Options remaining are B and C	35 Options remaining are A and B
16 Options remaining are A and C	36 Options remaining are A and D
17 Options remaining are B and D	37 Options remaining are A and D
18 Options remaining are A and B	38 Options remaining are B and C
19 Options remaining are B and C	39 Options remaining are A and C
20 Options remaining are B and C	40 Options remaining are A and D

50:50

41	Options remaining are A and D	47	Options remaining are A and D
42	Options remaining are A and B	48	Options remaining are C and D
43	Options remaining are B and D	49	Options remaining are C and D
44	Options remaining are A and C	50	Options remaining are C and D
45	Options remaining are B and D	51	Options remaining are A and D
46	Options remaining are A and B	52	Options remaining are A and B

£64,000

1	Options remaining are B and D	25	Options remaining are C and D
2	Options remaining are A and D	26	Options remaining are C and D
3	Options remaining are A and B	27	Options remaining are A and D
4	Options remaining are B and D	28	Options remaining are B and D
5	Options remaining are A and B	29	Options remaining are B and C
6	Options remaining are A and C	30	Options remaining are A and D
7	Options remaining are A and D	31	Options remaining are B and C
8	Options remaining are C and D	32	Options remaining are B and C
9	Options remaining are A and C	33	Options remaining are C and D
10	Options remaining are A and C	34	Options remaining are B and C
11	Options remaining are B and D	35	Options remaining are B and C
12	Options remaining are A and D	36	Options remaining are A and B
13	Options remaining are A and C	37	Options remaining are B and C
14	Options remaining are A and D	38	Options remaining are B and D
15	Options remaining are A and D	39	Options remaining are C and D
16	Options remaining are A and B	40	Options remaining are A and D
17	Options remaining are C and D	41	Options remaining are C and D
18	Options remaining are C and D	42	Options remaining are A and D
19	Options remaining are B and C	43	Options remaining are A and B
20	Options remaining are B and D	44	Options remaining are A and C
21	Options remaining are A and B	45	Options remaining are B and D
22	Options remaining are A and B	46	Options remaining are A and B
23	Options remaining are B and C	47	Options remaining are B and D
24	Options remaining are B and C	48	Options remaining are C and D

£125,000

1	Options remaining are A and B	6	Options remaining are B and C
2	Options remaining are C and D	7	Options remaining are A and C
3	Options remaining are C and D	8	Options remaining are A and D
4	Options remaining are A and C	9	Options remaining are A and B
5	Options remaining are B and D	10	Options remaining are A and C

50:50

11	Options remaining are A and C	28	Options remaining are A and B
12	Options remaining are B and C	29	Options remaining are C and D
13	Options remaining are B and C	30	Options remaining are B and C
14	Options remaining are B and D	31	Options remaining are A and C
15	Options remaining are C and D	32	Options remaining are A and B
16	Options remaining are A and B	33	Options remaining are B and C
17	Options remaining are C and D	34	Options remaining are A and C
18	Options remaining are A and B	35	Options remaining are A and C
19	Options remaining are A and B	36	Options remaining are A and B
20	Options remaining are A and C	37	Options remaining are B and D
21	Options remaining are B and D	38	Options remaining are B and C
22	Options remaining are C and D	39	Options remaining are A and B
23	Options remaining are C and D	40	Options remaining are B and C
24	Options remaining are A and B	41	Options remaining are A and D
25	Options remaining are A and D	42	Options remaining are C and D
26	Options remaining are A and B	43	Options remaining are A and B
27	Options remaining are A and B	44	Options remaining are A and C

£250,000

1	Options remaining are A and C	21	Options remaining are C and D
2	Options remaining are A and B	22	Options remaining are C and D
3	Options remaining are A and C	23	Options remaining are B and C
4	Options remaining are A and C	24	Options remaining are B and C
5	Options remaining are A and C	25	Options remaining are A and B
6	Options remaining are A and D	26	Options remaining are B and C
7	Options remaining are A and B	27	Options remaining are C and D
8	Options remaining are C and D	28	Options remaining are B and D
9	Options remaining are A and D	29	Options remaining are A and D
10	Options remaining are B and C	30	Options remaining are A and C
11	Options remaining are A and B	31	Options remaining are A and B
12	Options remaining are A and B	32	Options remaining are A and B
13	Options remaining are B and D	33	Options remaining are A and D
14	Options remaining are A and B	34	Options remaining are A and B
15	Options remaining are B and D	35	Options remaining are A and C
16	Options remaining are B and D	36	Options remaining are C and D
17	Options remaining are C and D	37	Options remaining are A and B
18	Options remaining are A and D	38	Options remaining are A and B
19	Options remaining are B and C	39	Options remaining are A and D
20	Options remaining are A and C	40	Options remaining are B and C

50:50

£500,000

1 Options remaining are B and C	19 Options remaining are B and C
2 Options remaining are B and C	20 Options remaining are C and D
3 Options remaining are A and B	21 Options remaining are B and D
4 Options remaining are A and B	22 Options remaining are A and C
5 Options remaining are A and C	23 Options remaining are B and D
6 Options remaining are A and B	24 Options remaining are B and D
7 Options remaining are A and C	25 Options remaining are A and C
8 Options remaining are B and C	26 Options remaining are C and D
9 Options remaining are A and C	27 Options remaining are A and D
10 Options remaining are A and D	28 Options remaining are A and C
11 Options remaining are B and C	29 Options remaining are C and D
12 Options remaining are B and C	30 Options remaining are A and B
13 Options remaining are A and B	31 Options remaining are A and B
14 Options remaining are A and C	32 Options remaining are A and B
15 Options remaining are C and D	33 Options remaining are A and C
16 Options remaining are A and C	34 Options remaining are A and D
17 Options remaining are A and C	35 Options remaining are A and B
18 Options remaining are A and B	36 Options remaining are B and D

£1,000,000

1 Options remaining are A and B	17 Options remaining are B and C
2 Options remaining are C and D	18 Options remaining are A and C
3 Options remaining are B and C	19 Options remaining are A and D
4 Options remaining are A and B	20 Options remaining are B and C
5 Options remaining are C and D	21 Options remaining are C and D
6 Options remaining are A and C	22 Options remaining are A and B
7 Options remaining are A and D	23 Options remaining are B and D
8 Options remaining are B and D	24 Options remaining are A and C
9 Options remaining are B and C	25 Options remaining are C and D
10 Options remaining are A and B	26 Options remaining are A and B
11 Options remaining are C and D	27 Options remaining are C and D
12 Options remaining are A and B	28 Options remaining are C and D
13 Options remaining are A and B	29 Options remaining are A and C
14 Options remaining are A and B	30 Options remaining are C and D
15 Options remaining are A and D	31 Options remaining are C and D
16 Options remaining are B and D	32 Options remaining are B and D

Ask The Audience

£100

#	A	B	C	D
1	A:0%	B:100%	C:0%	D:0%
2	A:0%	B:0%	C:0%	D:100%
3	A:0%	B:0%	C:100%	D:0%
4	A:0%	B:91%	C:9%	D:0%
5	A:100%	B:0%	C:0%	D:0%
6	A:0%	B:0%	C:0%	D:100%
7	A:0%	B:0%	C:0%	D:100%
8	A:95%	B:0%	C:5%	D:0%
9	A:91%	B:9%	C:0%	D:0%
10	A:0%	B:100%	C:0%	D:0%
11	A:0%	B:95%	C:5%	D:0%
12	A:0%	B:0%	C:100%	D:0%
13	A:0%	B:0%	C:0%	D:100%
14	A:0%	B:100%	C:0%	D:0%
15	A:100%	B:0%	C:0%	D:0%
16	A:0%	B:0%	C:0%	D:100%
17	A:0%	B:0%	C:100%	D:0%
18	A:0%	B:100%	C:0%	D:0%
19	A:0%	B:100%	C:0%	D:0%
20	A:0%	B:100%	C:0%	D:0%
21	A:0%	B:0%	C:0%	D:100%
22	A:0%	B:100%	C:0%	D:0%
23	A:100%	B:0%	C:0%	D:0%
24	A:91%	B:9%	C:0%	D:0%
25	A:0%	B:0%	C:0%	D:100%
26	A:0%	B:5%	C:5%	D:90%
27	A:0%	B:100%	C:0%	D:0%
28	A:100%	B:0%	C:0%	D:0%
29	A:0%	B:0%	C:100%	D:0%
30	A:100%	B:0%	C:0%	D:0%
31	A:5%	B:95%	C:0%	D:0%
32	A:0%	B:0%	C:100%	D:0%
33	A:0%	B:0%	C:0%	D:100%
34	A:100%	B:0%	C:0%	D:0%
35	A:0%	B:100%	C:0%	D:0%
36	A:0%	B:0%	C:100%	D:0%
37	A:0%	B:0%	C:0%	D:100%
38	A:100%	B:0%	C:0%	D:0%
39	A:20%	B:10%	C:70%	D:0%
40	A:100%	B:0%	C:0%	D:0%
41	A:0%	B:0%	C:100%	D:0%
42	A:0%	B:100%	C:0%	D:0%
43	A:0%	B:0%	C:100%	D:0%
44	A:0%	B:0%	C:0%	D:100%
45	A:0%	B:81%	C:5%	D:14%
46	A:0%	B:100%	C:0%	D:0%
47	A:0%	B:0%	C:0%	D:100%
48	A:0%	B:0%	C:100%	D:0%
49	A:5%	B:14%	C:0%	D:81%
50	A:0%	B:0%	C:0%	D:100%
51	A:5%	B:95%	C:0%	D:0%
52	A:0%	B:0%	C:100%	D:0%
53	A:0%	B:0%	C:100%	D:0%
54	A:5%	B:0%	C:95%	D:0%
55	A:0%	B:0%	C:0%	D:100%
56	A:100%	B:0%	C:0%	D:0%
57	A:0%	B:0%	C:0%	D:100%
58	A:0%	B:0%	C:5%	D:95%
59	A:0%	B:0%	C:0%	D:100%
60	A:0%	B:100%	C:0%	D:0%
61	A:0%	B:100%	C:0%	D:0%
62	A:100%	B:0%	C:0%	D:0%
63	A:0%	B:5%	C:0%	D:95%
64	A:0%	B:0%	C:0%	D:100%
65	A:100%	B:0%	C:0%	D:0%
66	A:0%	B:5%	C:95%	D:0%
67	A:100%	B:0%	C:0%	D:0%
68	A:0%	B:0%	C:86%	D:14%
69	A:0%	B:0%	C:0%	D:100%
70	A:0%	B:0%	C:100%	D:0%
71	A:0%	B:0%	C:100%	D:0%
72	A:5%	B:0%	C:90%	D:5%
73	A:100%	B:0%	C:0%	D:0%
74	A:0%	B:19%	C:0%	D:81%

ASK THE AUDIENCE

75	A:0%	B:100%	C:0%	D:0%	82	A:100%	B:0%	C:0%	D:0%
76	A:0%	B:0%	C:0%	D:100%	83	A:0%	B:0%	C:100%	D:0%
77	A:5%	B:67%	C:18%	D:10%	84	A:95%	B:0%	C:5%	D:0%
78	A:0%	B:100%	C:0%	D:0%	85	A:37%	B:5%	C:10%	D:48%
79	A:0%	B:100%	C:0%	D:0%	86	A:0%	B:0%	C:0%	D:100%
80	A:100%	B:0%	C:0%	D:0%	87	A:100%	B:0%	C:0%	D:0%
81	A:100%	B:0%	C:0%	D:0%	88	A:0%	B:0%	C:5%	D:95%

£200

1	A:0%	B:14%	C:86%	D:0%	33	A:0%	B:0%	C:100%	D:0%
2	A:0%	B:100%	C:0%	D:0%	34	A:100%	B:0%	C:0%	D:0%
3	A:0%	B:100%	C:0%	D:0%	35	A:0%	B:100%	C:0%	D:0%
4	A:100%	B:0%	C:0%	D:0%	36	A:0%	B:100%	C:0%	D:0%
5	A:0%	B:0%	C:100%	D:0%	37	A:0%	B:0%	C:0%	D:100%
6	A:0%	B:0%	C:0%	D:100%	38	A:0%	B:0%	C:100%	D:0%
7	A:0%	B:100%	C:0%	D:0%	39	A:100%	B:0%	C:0%	D:0%
8	A:0%	B:100%	C:0%	D:0%	40	A:0%	B:10%	C:90%	D:0%
9	A:0%	B:0%	C:0%	D:100%	41	A:90%	B:10%	C:0%	D:0%
10	A:0%	B:0%	C:100%	D:0%	42	A:0%	B:100%	C:0%	D:0%
11	A:0%	B:100%	C:0%	D:0%	43	A:0%	B:0%	C:0%	D:100%
12	A:0%	B:100%	C:0%	D:0%	44	A:5%	B:0%	C:0%	D:95%
13	A:95%	B:5%	C:0%	D:0%	45	A:0%	B:100%	C:0%	D:0%
14	A:5%	B:5%	C:0%	D:90%	46	A:14%	B:86%	C:0%	D:0%
15	A:0%	B:95%	C:0%	D:5%	47	A:28%	B:10%	C:5%	D:57%
16	A:0%	B:100%	C:0%	D:0%	48	A:0%	B:0%	C:100%	D:0%
17	A:0%	B:0%	C:0%	D:100%	49	A:0%	B:0%	C:0%	D:100%
18	A:0%	B:100%	C:0%	D:0%	50	A:10%	B:90%	C:0%	D:0%
19	A:100%	B:0%	C:0%	D:0%	51	A:5%	B:0%	C:95%	D:0%
20	A:5%	B:5%	C:0%	D:90%	52	A:0%	B:0%	C:0%	D:100%
21	A:0%	B:5%	C:95%	D:0%	53	A:14%	B:86%	C:0%	D:0%
22	A:100%	B:0%	C:0%	D:0%	54	A:71%	B:5%	C:5%	D:19%
23	A:0%	B:100%	C:0%	D:0%	55	A:0%	B:100%	C:0%	D:0%
24	A:0%	B:100%	C:0%	D:0%	56	A:0%	B:100%	C:0%	D:0%
25	A:0%	B:0%	C:0%	D:100%	57	A:0%	B:0%	C:100%	D:0%
26	A:0%	B:100%	C:0%	D:0%	58	A:0%	B:100%	C:0%	D:0%
27	A:0%	B:100%	C:0%	D:0%	59	A:100%	B:0%	C:0%	D:0%
28	A:0%	B:95%	C:5%	D:0%	60	A:0%	B:5%	C:95%	D:0%
29	A:0%	B:0%	C:0%	D:100%	61	A:0%	B:0%	C:0%	D:100%
30	A:10%	B:90%	C:0%	D:0%	62	A:0%	B:0%	C:0%	D:100%
31	A:0%	B:0%	C:0%	D:100%	63	A:0%	B:5%	C:0%	D:95%
32	A:28%	B:10%	C:62%	D:0%	64	A:0%	B:0%	C:0%	D:100%

65	A:0%	B:0%	C:100%	D:0%
66	A:85%	B:0%	C:5%	D:10%
67	A:100%	B:0%	C:0%	D:0%
68	A:0%	B:100%	C:0%	D:0%
69	A:0%	B:5%	C:0%	D:95%
70	A:0%	B:95%	C:0%	D:5%
71	A:14%	B:76%	C:10%	D:0%
72	A:14%	B:86%	C:0%	D:0%
73	A:0%	B:100%	C:0%	D:0%
74	A:0%	B:100%	C:0%	D:0%
75	A:5%	B:95%	C:0%	D:0%
76	A:0%	B:0%	C:100%	D:0%
77	A:0%	B:100%	C:0%	D:0%
78	A:0%	B:100%	C:0%	D:0%
79	A:0%	B:81%	C:0%	D:19%
80	A:0%	B:0%	C:0%	D:100%
81	A:0%	B:0%	C:100%	D:0%
82	A:90%	B:10%	C:0%	D:0%
83	A:0%	B:0%	C:100%	D:0%
84	A:0%	B:0%	C:100%	D:0%

£300

1	A:0%	B:0%	C:100%	D:0%
2	A:80%	B:10%	C:0%	D:10%
3	A:0%	B:0%	C:5%	D:95%
4	A:0%	B:0%	C:100%	D:0%
5	A:0%	B:0%	C:5%	D:95%
6	A:100%	B:0%	C:0%	D:0%
7	A:100%	B:0%	C:0%	D:0%
8	A:100%	B:0%	C:0%	D:0%
9	A:0%	B:100%	C:0%	D:0%
10	A:95%	B:0%	C:0%	D:5%
11	A:0%	B:0%	C:0%	D:100%
12	A:95%	B:0%	C:0%	D:5%
13	A:0%	B:0%	C:100%	D:0%
14	A:100%	B:0%	C:0%	D:0%
15	A:0%	B:95%	C:0%	D:5%
16	A:0%	B:0%	C:100%	D:0%
17	A:0%	B:100%	C:0%	D:0%
18	A:0%	B:100%	C:0%	D:0%
19	A:0%	B:100%	C:0%	D:0%
20	A:95%	B:0%	C:5%	D:0%
21	A:0%	B:0%	C:100%	D:0%
22	A:80%	B:15%	C:5%	D:0%
23	A:0%	B:5%	C:0%	D:95%
24	A:0%	B:0%	C:0%	D:100%
25	A:0%	B:0%	C:95%	D:5%
26	A:95%	B:0%	C:0%	D:5%
27	A:5%	B:90%	C:0%	D:5%
28	A:0%	B:0%	C:100%	D:0%
29	A:0%	B:100%	C:0%	D:0%
30	A:100%	B:0%	C:0%	D:0%
31	A:10%	B:0%	C:5%	D:85%
32	A:100%	B:0%	C:0%	D:0%
33	A:0%	B:95%	C:0%	D:5%
34	A:0%	B:0%	C:100%	D:0%
35	A:0%	B:0%	C:0%	D:100%
36	A:0%	B:67%	C:0%	D:33%
37	A:100%	B:0%	C:0%	D:0%
38	A:0%	B:100%	C:0%	D:0%
39	A:0%	B:71%	C:24%	D:5%
40	A:0%	B:0%	C:100%	D:0%
41	A:15%	B:85%	C:0%	D:0%
42	A:100%	B:0%	C:0%	D:0%
43	A:100%	B:0%	C:0%	D:0%
44	A:15%	B:0%	C:85%	D:0%
45	A:0%	B:100%	C:0%	D:0%
46	A:0%	B:0%	C:100%	D:0%
47	A:0%	B:100%	C:0%	D:0%
48	A:0%	B:100%	C:0%	D:0%
49	A:95%	B:5%	C:0%	D:0%
50	A:0%	B:71%	C:19%	D:10%
51	A:0%	B:0%	C:100%	D:0%
52	A:0%	B:95%	C:0%	D:5%
53	A:67%	B:0%	C:57%	D:13%
54	A:15%	B:0%	C:0%	D:85%
55	A:24%	B:0%	C:57%	D:13%
56	A:5%	B:10%	C:80%	D:5%
57	A:5%	B:90%	C:0%	D:5%
58	A:5%	B:10%	C:0%	D:85%

ASK THE AUDIENCE

59	A:95%	B:0%	C:5%	D:0%		70	A:0%	B:5%	C:0%	D:95%
60	A:95%	B:0%	C:0%	D:5%		71	A:0%	B:90%	C:10%	D:0%
61	A:5%	B:50%	C:40%	D:5%		72	A:0%	B:95%	C:5%	D:0%
62	A:0%	B:10%	C:5%	D:85%		73	A:10%	B:67%	C:10%	D:13%
63	A:0%	B:0%	C:10%	D:90%		74	A:0%	B:10%	C:5%	D:85%
64	A:0%	B:100%	C:0%	D:0%		75	A:0%	B:95%	C:0%	D:5%
65	A:0%	B:0%	C:5%	D:95%		76	A:0%	B:0%	C:0%	D:100%
66	A:0%	B:0%	C:5%	D:95%		77	A:0%	B:0%	C:100%	D:0%
67	A:5%	B:90%	C:0%	D:5%		78	A:5%	B:95%	C:0%	D:0%
68	A:95%	B:0%	C:0%	D:5%		79	A:0%	B:100%	C:0%	D:0%
69	A:0%	B:5%	C:14%	D:81%		80	A:19%	B:76%	C:0%	D:5%

£500

1	A:95%	B:0%	C:5%	D:0%		28	A:57%	B:10%	C:33%	D:0%
2	A:10%	B:80%	C:10%	D:%		29	A:95%	B:0%	C:0%	D:5%
3	A:80%	B:5%	C:5%	D:10%		30	A:0%	B:0%	C:95%	D:5%
4	A:0%	B:0%	C:100%	D:0%		31	A:90%	B:5%	C:0%	D:5%
5	A:70%	B:15%	C:15%	D:0%		32	A:90%	B:5%	C:0%	D:5%
6	A:0%	B:100%	C:0%	D:0%		33	A:5%	B:15%	C:75%	D:5%
7	A:52%	B:0%	C:5%	D:43%		34	A:0%	B:5%	C:95%	D:0%
8	A:28%	B:62%	C:5%	D:5%		35	A:5%	B:0%	C:28%	D:67%
9	A:15%	B:5%	C:80%	D:0%		36	A:10%	B:85%	C:5%	D:0%
10	A:0%	B:0%	C:100%	D:0%		37	A:95%	B:0%	C:0%	D:5%
11	A:0%	B:90%	C:5%	D:5%		38	A:100%	B:0%	C:0%	D:0%
12	A:5%	B:57%	C:38%	D:0%		39	A:0%	B:90%	C:5%	D:5%
13	A:5%	B:95%	C:0%	D:0%		40	A:0%	B:5%	C:5%	D:90%
14	A:100%	B:0%	C:0%	D:0%		41	A:0%	B:90%	C:10%	D:0%
15	A:0%	B:0%	C:100%	D:0%		42	A:0%	B:0%	C:90%	D:10%
16	A:5%	B:5%	C:15%	D:75%		43	A:0%	B:0%	C:100%	D:0%
17	A:100%	B:0%	C:0%	D:0%		44	A:5%	B:0%	C:5%	D:90%
18	A:100%	B:0%	C:0%	D:0%		45	A:67%	B:23%	C:10%	D:0%
19	A:0%	B:80%	C:15%	D:5%		46	A:0%	B:95%	C:5%	D:0%
20	A:38%	B:52%	C:5%	D:5%		47	A:0%	B:75%	C:10%	D:15%
21	A:15%	B:5%	C:5%	D:75%		48	A:90%	B:5%	C:5%	D:0%
22	A:0%	B:0%	C:0%	D:100%		49	A:0%	B:0%	C:5%	D:95%
23	A:0%	B:100%	C:0%	D:0%		50	A:0%	B:5%	C:0%	D:95%
24	A:10%	B:85%	C:0%	D:5%		51	A:0%	B:5%	C:95%	D:0%
25	A:5%	B:5%	C:90%	D:0%		52	A:0%	B:10%	C:85%	D:5%
26	A:0%	B:0%	C:10%	D:90%		53	A:0%	B:95%	C:5%	D:0%
27	A:90%	B:5%	C:5%	D:0%		54	A:80%	B:0%	C:10%	D:10%

ASK THE AUDIENCE

55	A:0%	B:5%	C:95%	D:0%	66	A:0%	B:0%	C:100%	D:0%
56	A:0%	B:95%	C:0%	D:5%	67	A:0%	B:95%	C:0%	D:5%
57	A:5%	B:0%	C:5%	D:90%	68	A:0%	B:100%	C:0%	D:0%
58	A:0%	B:0%	C:100%	D:0%	69	A:15%	B:0%	C:85%	D:0%
59	A:0%	B:0%	C:0%	D:100%	70	A:90%	B:5%	C:0%	D:5%
60	A:5%	B:10%	C:23%	D:62%	71	A:0%	B:0%	C:100%	D:0%
61	A:19%	B:0%	C:71%	D:10%	72	A:0%	B:5%	C:0%	D:95%
62	A:33%	B:15%	C:0%	D:52%	73	A:90%	B:0%	C:5%	D:5%
63	A:10%	B:5%	C:85%	D:0%	74	A:100%	B:0%	C:0%	D:0%
64	A:0%	B:5%	C:95%	D:0%	75	A:0%	B:0%	C:0%	D:100%
65	A:5%	B:80%	C:5%	D:10%	76	A:0%	B:100%	C:0%	D:0%

£1,000

1	A:5%	B:90%	C:0%	D:5%	29	A:20%	B:10%	C:70%	D:0%
2	A:0%	B:20%	C:0%	D:80%	30	A:90%	B:0%	C:0%	D:10%
3	A:10%	B:75%	C:10%	D:5%	31	A:25%	B:70%	C:5%	D:0%
4	A:5%	B:0%	C:0%	D:95%	32	A:5%	B:5%	C:80%	D:10%
5	A:0%	B:0%	C:5%	D:95%	33	A:5%	B:75%	C:10%	D:10%
6	A:80%	B:0%	C:20%	D:0%	34	A:15%	B:0%	C:0%	D:85%
7	A:0%	B:0%	C:0%	D:100%	35	A:0%	B:0%	C:0%	D:100%
8	A:0%	B:0%	C:100%	D:0%	36	A:5%	B:95%	C:0%	D:0%
9	A:0%	B:0%	C:5%	D:95%	37	A:28%	B:0%	C:5%	D:67%
10	A:5%	B:95%	C:0%	D:0%	38	A:0%	B:0%	C:0%	D:100%
11	A:10%	B:5%	C:80%	D:5%	39	A:10%	B:90%	C:0%	D:0%
12	A:0%	B:0%	C:100%	D:0%	40	A:0%	B:0%	C:100%	D:0%
13	A:10%	B:10%	C:14%	D:66%	41	A:0%	B:33%	C:10%	D:57%
14	A:0%	B:5%	C:95%	D:0%	42	A:5%	B:0%	C:0%	D:95%
15	A:0%	B:100%	C:0%	D:0%	43	A:0%	B:0%	C:100%	D:0%
16	A:100%	B:0%	C:0%	D:0%	44	A:0%	B:25%	C:5%	D:70%
17	A:95%	B:0%	C:0%	D:5%	45	A:5%	B:5%	C:90%	D:0%
18	A:0%	B:0%	C:0%	D:100%	46	A:0%	B:95%	C:0%	D:5%
19	A:20%	B:0%	C:0%	D:80%	47	A:0%	B:5%	C:95%	D:0%
20	A:0%	B:80%	C:10%	D:10%	48	A:0%	B:5%	C:95%	D:0%
21	A:5%	B:90%	C:0%	D:5%	49	A:5%	B:10%	C:85%	D:0%
22	A:5%	B:57%	C:33%	D:5%	50	A:5%	B:5%	C:0%	D:90%
23	A:24%	B:76%	C:0%	D:0%	51	A:95%	B:0%	C:5%	D:0%
24	A:5%	B:20%	C:0%	D:75%	52	A:19%	B:28%	C:15%	D:38%
25	A:38%	B:0%	C:62%	D:0%	53	A:5%	B:95%	C:0%	D:0%
26	A:70%	B:15%	C:15%	D:0%	54	A:23%	B:0%	C:10%	D:67%
27	A:24%	B:24%	C:52%	D:0%	55	A:100%	B:0%	C:0%	D:0%
28	A:10%	B:0%	C:0%	D:90%	56	A:0%	B:0%	C:0%	D:100%

ASK THE AUDIENCE

57	A:15%	B:0%	C:37%	D:48%	65	A:25%	B:5%	C:0%	D:70%
58	A:0%	B:80%	C:15%	D:5%	66	A:38%	B:0%	C:15%	D:47%
59	A:15%	B:75%	C:10%	D:0%	67	A:60%	B:15%	C:15%	D:10%
60	A:70%	B:0%	C:0%	D:30%	68	A:20%	B:0%	C:5%	D:75%
61	A:14%	B:10%	C:71%	D:5%	69	A:0%	B:0%	C:0%	D:100%
62	A:0%	B:100%	C:0%	D:0%	70	A:5%	B:90%	C:0%	D:5%
63	A:80%	B:20%	C:0%	D:0%	71	A:0%	B:95%	C:0%	D:5%
64	A:0%	B:100%	C:0%	D:0%	72	A:0%	B:100%	C:0%	D:0%

£2,000

1	A:52%	B:43%	C:5%	D:0%	32	A:70%	B:0%	C:15%	D:15%
2	A:5%	B:5%	C:20%	D:70%	33	A:10%	B:5%	C:10%	D:75%
3	A:10%	B:0%	C:70%	D:20%	34	A:33%	B:0%	C:19%	D:48%
4	A:5%	B:5%	C:0%	D:90%	35	A:19%	B:76%	C:0%	D:5%
5	A:5%	B:5%	C:38%	D:52%	36	A:10%	B:90%	C:0%	D:0%
6	A:15%	B:65%	C:5%	D:15%	37	A:5%	B:5%	C:62%	D:28%
7	A:5%	B:10%	C:70%	D:15%	38	A:10%	B:5%	C:0%	D:85%
8	A:95%	B:5%	C:0%	D:0%	39	A:52%	B:15%	C:15%	D:18%
9	A:0%	B:0%	C:100%	D:0%	40	A:5%	B:0%	C:5%	D:90%
10	A:10%	B:5%	C:0%	D:85%	41	A:90%	B:5%	C:0%	D:5%
11	A:28%	B:5%	C:62%	D:5%	42	A:5%	B:0%	C:10%	D:85%
12	A:95%	B:0%	C:0%	D:5%	43	A:15%	B:0%	C:19%	D:66%
13	A:5%	B:90%	C:0%	D:5%	44	A:15%	B:80%	C:5%	D:0%
14	A:80%	B:15%	C:5%	D:0%	45	A:62%	B:5%	C:15%	D:18%
15	A:10%	B:10%	C:80%	D:0%	46	A:15%	B:43%	C:37%	D:5%
16	A:85%	B:15%	C:0%	D:0%	47	A:0%	B:10%	C:5%	D:85%
17	A:15%	B:85%	C:0%	D:0%	48	A:5%	B:0%	C:0%	D:95%
18	A:5%	B:90%	C:5%	D:0%	49	A:5%	B:19%	C:19%	D:57%
19	A:24%	B:5%	C:19%	D:52%	50	A:10%	B:38%	C:10%	D:42%
20	A:80%	B:10%	C:10%	D:0%	51	A:10%	B:5%	C:85%	D:0%
21	A:67%	B:28%	C:5%	D:0%	52	A:42%	B:29%	C:0%	D:29%
22	A:10%	B:10%	C:0%	D:80%	53	A:85%	B:10%	C:0%	D:5%
23	A:5%	B:52%	C:38%	D:5%	54	A:15%	B:10%	C:65%	D:10%
24	A:23%	B:62%	C:5%	D:10%	55	A:95%	B:5%	C:0%	D:0%
25	A:15%	B:0%	C:80%	D:5%	56	A:0%	B:5%	C:95%	D:0%
26	A:0%	B:95%	C:5%	D:0%	57	A:10%	B:5%	C:85%	D:0%
27	A:25%	B:5%	C:0%	D:70%	58	A:0%	B:33%	C:48%	D:19%
28	A:0%	B:10%	C:0%	D:90%	59	A:5%	B:5%	C:0%	D:90%
29	A:10%	B:5%	C:65%	D:20%	60	A:0%	B:5%	C:5%	D:90%
30	A:70%	B:15%	C:15%	D:0%	61	A:10%	B:48%	C:0%	D:42%
31	A:10%	B:5%	C:80%	D:5%	62	A:10%	B:20%	C:10%	D:60%

ASK THE AUDIENCE

63	A:5%	B:80%	C:15%	D:0%	66	A:0%	B:0%	C:0%	D:100%
64	A:10%	B:10%	C:80%	D:0%	67	A:0%	B:0%	C:5%	D:95%
65	A:15%	B:52%	C:0%	D:33%	68	A:0%	B:0%	C:0%	D:100%

£4,000

1	A:4%	B:92%	C:0%	D:4%	33	A:74%	B:18%	C:4%	D:4%
2	A:8%	B:0%	C:92%	D:0%	34	A:30%	B:35%	C:5%	D:30%
3	A:4%	B:92%	C:0%	D:4%	35	A:17%	B:30%	C:48%	D:5%
4	A:8%	B:74%	C:18%	D:0%	36	A:22%	B:13%	C:0%	D:65%
5	A:82%	B:18%	C:0%	D:0%	37	A:74%	B:18%	C:8%	D:0%
6	A:4%	B:82%	C:10%	D:4%	38	A:0%	B:0%	C:100%	D:0%
7	A:35%	B:17%	C:0%	D:48%	39	A:0%	B:100%	C:0%	D:0%
8	A:4%	B:75%	C:17%	D:4%	40	A:26%	B:4%	C:57%	D:13%
9	A:0%	B:9%	C:30%	D:61%	41	A:4%	B:18%	C:0%	D:78%
10	A:22%	B:4%	C:52%	D:22%	42	A:13%	B:39%	C:13%	D:35%
11	A:0%	B:0%	C:100%	D:0%	43	A:9%	B:91%	C:0%	D:0%
12	A:17%	B:13%	C:70%	D:0%	44	A:4%	B:87%	C:9%	D:0%
13	A:0%	B:35%	C:61%	D:4%	45	A:17%	B:22%	C:7%	D:54%
14	A:13%	B:13%	C:17%	D:57%	46	A:22%	B:0%	C:56%	D:22%
15	A:61%	B:35%	C:0%	D:4%	47	A:78%	B:22%	C:0%	D:0%
16	A:79%	B:7%	C:7%	D:7%	48	A:0%	B:0%	C:87%	D:13%
17	A:7%	B:70%	C:23%	D:0%	49	A:0%	B:4%	C:18%	D:78%
18	A:35%	B:61%	C:4%	D:0%	50	A:4%	B:96%	C:0%	D:0%
19	A:0%	B:26%	C:61%	D:13%	51	A:0%	B:96%	C:0%	D:4%
20	A:26%	B:70%	C:4%	D:0%	52	A:0%	B:0%	C:96%	D:4%
21	A:7%	B:13%	C:57%	D:23%	53	A:4%	B:78%	C:18%	D:0%
22	A:22%	B:4%	C:52%	D:22%	54	A:0%	B:4%	C:92%	D:4%
23	A:70%	B:30%	C:0%	D:0%	55	A:8%	B:5%	C:5%	D:82%
24	A:4%	B:96%	C:0%	D:0%	56	A:0%	B:13%	C:22%	D:65%
25	A:0%	B:0%	C:96%	D:4%	57	A:26%	B:26%	C:31%	D:17%
26	A:0%	B:82%	C:0%	D:18%	58	A:0%	B:87%	C:13%	D:0%
27	A:8%	B:0%	C:13%	D:78%	59	A:7%	B:17%	C:52%	D:24%
28	A:40%	B:7%	C:53%	D:0%	60	A:4%	B:92%	C:4%	D:0%
29	A:4%	B:4%	C:92%	D:0%	61	A:18%	B:0%	C:82%	D:0%
30	A:100%	B:0%	C:0%	D:0%	62	A:0%	B:4%	C:4%	D:92%
31	A:65%	B:7%	C:0%	D:28%	63	A:0%	B:0%	C:100%	D:0%
32	A:87%	B:0%	C:8%	D:5%	64	A:13%	B:57%	C:22%	D:8%

ASK THE AUDIENCE

£8,000

1	A:0%	B:22%	C:43%	D:35%	31	A:7%	B:0%	C:74%	D:19%
2	A:17%	B:73%	C:10%	D:0%	32	A:7%	B:57%	C:4%	D:32%
3	A:10%	B:0%	C:16%	D:74%	33	A:17%	B:0%	C:13%	D:70%
4	A:0%	B:0%	C:26%	D:74%	34	A:0%	B:26%	C:74%	D:0%
5	A:0%	B:74%	C:10%	D:16%	35	A:35%	B:4%	C:57%	D:4%
6	A:0%	B:22%	C:13%	D:65%	36	A:7%	B:74%	C:4%	D:15%
7	A:73%	B:22%	C:5%	D:0%	37	A:30%	B:65%	C:0%	D:5%
8	A:26%	B:59%	C:5%	D:10%	38	A:35%	B:7%	C:43%	D:15%
9	A:10%	B:63%	C:10%	D:17%	39	A:39%	B:39%	C:22%	D:0%
10	A:4%	B:63%	C:7%	D:26%	40	A:57%	B:23%	C:13%	D:7%
11	A:65%	B:7%	C:14%	D:14%	41	A:4%	B:13%	C:17%	D:66%
12	A:5%	B:43%	C:9%	D:43%	42	A:17%	B:23%	C:30%	D:30%
13	A:0%	B:56%	C:22%	D:22%	43	A:8%	B:0%	C:87%	D:5%
14	A:35%	B:39%	C:4%	D:22%	44	A:30%	B:30%	C:14%	D:26%
15	A:4%	B:74%	C:22%	D:0%	45	A:13%	B:66%	C:8%	D:13%
16	A:35%	B:17%	C:18%	D:30%	46	A:52%	B:22%	C:7%	D:19%
17	A:0%	B:39%	C:48%	D:13%	47	A:52%	B:14%	C:17%	D:17%
18	A:13%	B:4%	C:66%	D:17%	48	A:0%	B:87%	C:8%	D:5%
19	A:84%	B:8%	C:8%	D:0%	49	A:70%	B:4%	C:4%	D:22%
20	A:0%	B:65%	C:4%	D:31%	50	A:26%	B:48%	C:13%	D:13%
21	A:70%	B:17%	C:9%	D:4%	51	A:9%	B:39%	C:26%	D:26%
22	A:13%	B:75%	C:7%	D:5%	52	A:17%	B:13%	C:61%	D:9%
23	A:74%	B:7%	C:15%	D:4%	53	A:4%	B:48%	C:17%	D:31%
24	A:65%	B:13%	C:22%	D:0%	54	A:13%	B:65%	C:4%	D:18%
25	A:78%	B:0%	C:22%	D:0%	55	A:17%	B:0%	C:17%	D:66%
26	A:0%	B:61%	C:22%	D:17%	56	A:30%	B:35%	C:13%	D:22%
27	A:4%	B:13%	C:52%	D:31%	57	A:13%	B:7%	C:7%	D:73%
28	A:43%	B:14%	C:35%	D:8%	58	A:0%	B:4%	C:0%	D:96%
29	A:13%	B:22%	C:61%	D:4%	59	A:6%	B:7%	C:0%	D:87%
30	A:22%	B:22%	C:13%	D:43%	60	A:30%	B:39%	C:0%	D:31%

£16,000

1	A:22%	B:0%	C:39%	D:39%	9	A:0%	B:5%	C:90%	D:5%
2	A:4%	B:0%	C:96%	D:0%	10	A:25%	B:39%	C:18%	D:18%
3	A:17%	B:0%	C:57%	D:26%	11	A:4%	B:70%	C:0%	D:26%
4	A:57%	B:4%	C:4%	D:35%	12	A:7%	B:0%	C:4%	D:89%
5	A:13%	B:13%	C:57%	D:17%	13	A:4%	B:22%	C:26%	D:48%
6	A:0%	B:7%	C:61%	D:32%	14	A:65%	B:22%	C:5%	D:8%
7	A:22%	B:17%	C:48%	D:13%	15	A:4%	B:87%	C:9%	D:0%
8	A:43%	B:39%	C:0%	D:18%	16	A:13%	B:61%	C:13%	D:13%

ASK THE AUDIENCE

#	A	B	C	D
17	A:0%	B:39%	C:22%	D:39%
18	A:0%	B:78%	C:5%	D:17%
19	A:9%	B:0%	C:82%	D:9%
20	A:4%	B:82%	C:10%	D:4%
21	A:8%	B:26%	C:61%	D:5%
22	A:48%	B:0%	C:22%	D:30%
23	A:0%	B:17%	C:26%	D:57%
24	A:8%	B:87%	C:5%	D:0%
25	A:8%	B:57%	C:35%	D:0%
26	A:0%	B:0%	C:91%	D:9%
27	A:39%	B:35%	C:4%	D:22%
28	A:4%	B:17%	C:57%	D:22%
29	A:4%	B:0%	C:57%	D:39%
30	A:57%	B:22%	C:17%	D:4%
31	A:17%	B:22%	C:18%	D:43%
32	A:4%	B:0%	C:70%	D:26%
33	A:8%	B:5%	C:87%	D:0%
34	A:0%	B:87%	C:5%	D:8%
35	A:74%	B:0%	C:13%	D:13%
36	A:13%	B:57%	C:17%	D:13%
37	A:26%	B:17%	C:0%	D:57%
38	A:43%	B:35%	C:0%	D:22%
39	A:8%	B:13%	C:5%	D:74%
40	A:0%	B:8%	C:87%	D:5%
41	A:65%	B:22%	C:5%	D:8%
42	A:23%	B:17%	C:17%	D:43%
43	A:39%	B:57%	C:4%	D:0%
44	A:5%	B:22%	C:65%	D:8%
45	A:13%	B:52%	C:30%	D:5%
46	A:5%	B:30%	C:13%	D:52%
47	A:5%	B:78%	C:12%	D:5%
48	A:8%	B:87%	C:5%	D:0%
49	A:39%	B:22%	C:39%	D:0%
50	A:43%	B:0%	C:43%	D:14%
51	A:60%	B:29%	C:11%	D:10%
52	A:39%	B:57%	C:0%	D:4%
53	A:5%	B:8%	C:65%	D:22%
54	A:20%	B:11%	C:39%	D:30%
55	A:4%	B:82%	C:10%	D:4%
56	A:5%	B:16%	C:74%	D:5%

£32,000

#	A	B	C	D
1	A:27%	B:59%	C:5%	D:9%
2	A:36%	B:32%	C:27%	D:5%
3	A:5%	B:90%	C:0%	D:5%
4	A:27%	B:18%	C:5%	D:50%
5	A:64%	B:5%	C:13%	D:18%
6	A:18%	B:14%	C:14%	D:54%
7	A:8%	B:5%	C:5%	D:82%
8	A:13%	B:23%	C:23%	D:41%
9	A:5%	B:5%	C:90%	D:0%
10	A:32%	B:64%	C:4%	D:0%
11	A:45%	B:14%	C:5%	D:36%
12	A:100%	B:0%	C:0%	D:0%
13	A:45%	B:5%	C:27%	D:23%
14	A:9%	B:32%	C:50%	D:9%
15	A:5%	B:27%	C:27%	D:41%
16	A:14%	B:0%	C:77%	D:9%
17	A:0%	B:27%	C:5%	D:68%
18	A:41%	B:41%	C:0%	D:18%
19	A:9%	B:14%	C:73%	D:4%
20	A:18%	B:36%	C:32%	D:14%
21	A:36%	B:14%	C:18%	D:32%
22	A:41%	B:0%	C:50%	D:9%
23	A:14%	B:4%	C:59%	D:23%
24	A:41%	B:27%	C:27%	D:5%
25	A:23%	B:59%	C:9%	D:9%
26	A:22%	B:50%	C:14%	D:14%
27	A:9%	B:27%	C:0%	D:64%
28	A:0%	B:23%	C:18%	D:59%
29	A:5%	B:50%	C:5%	D:40%
30	A:9%	B:27%	C:50%	D:14%
31	A:4%	B:14%	C:50%	D:32%
32	A:86%	B:0%	C:0%	D:14%
33	A:41%	B:23%	C:13%	D:23%
34	A:0%	B:55%	C:9%	D:36%
35	A:46%	B:9%	C:36%	D:9%
36	A:68%	B:0%	C:9%	D:23%
37	A:32%	B:13%	C:23%	D:32%
38	A:0%	B:27%	C:55%	D:18%

	A	B	C	D		A	B	C	D
39	A:41%	B:4%	C:14%	D:41%	46	A:14%	B:32%	C:40%	D:14%
40	A:18%	B:23%	C:0%	D:59%	47	A:4%	B:14%	C:18%	D:64%
41	A:9%	B:0%	C:27%	D:64%	48	A:27%	B:23%	C:23%	D:27%
42	A:14%	B:86%	C:0%	D:0%	49	A:13%	B:32%	C:55%	D:0%
43	A:14%	B:55%	C:4%	D:27%	50	A:0%	B:9%	C:91%	D:0%
44	A:36%	B:45%	C:19%	D:0%	51	A:36%	B:0%	C:28%	D:36%
45	A:0%	B:23%	C:23%	D:54%	52	A:9%	B:91%	C:0%	D:0%

£64,000

	A	B	C	D		A	B	C	D
1	A:14%	B:27%	C:32%	D:27%	25	A:18%	B:50%	C:18%	D:14%
2	A:14%	B:32%	C:27%	D:27%	26	A:0%	B:14%	C:68%	D:18%
3	A:8%	B:23%	C:55%	D:14%	27	A:68%	B:14%	C:14%	D:4%
4	A:5%	B:18%	C:32%	D:45%	28	A:18%	B:27%	C:0%	D:55%
5	A:23%	B:32%	C:41%	D:5%	29	A:9%	B:32%	C:32%	D:27%
6	A:41%	B:5%	C:45%	D:9%	30	A:26%	B:5%	C:5%	D:64%
7	A:41%	B:5%	C:0%	D:54%	31	A:0%	B:55%	C:32%	D:13%
8	A:9%	B:5%	C:59%	D:27%	32	A:27%	B:18%	C:41%	D:14%
9	A:27%	B:5%	C:45%	D:23%	33	A:41%	B:18%	C:9%	D:32%
10	A:4%	B:41%	C:55%	D:0%	34	A:23%	B:9%	C:68%	D:0%
11	A:27%	B:19%	C:45%	D:9%	35	A:0%	B:55%	C:4%	D:41%
12	A:54%	B:23%	C:0%	D:23%	36	A:32%	B:9%	C:36%	D:23%
13	A:9%	B:27%	C:32%	D:32%	37	A:27%	B:27%	C:23%	D:23%
14	A:9%	B:45%	C:32%	D:14%	38	A:23%	B:23%	C:45%	D:9%
15	A:46%	B:27%	C:0%	D:27%	39	A:9%	B:32%	C:14%	D:45%
16	A:78%	B:4%	C:4%	D:14%	40	A:23%	B:27%	C:23%	D:27%
17	A:28%	B:36%	C:18%	D:18%	41	A:18%	B:27%	C:10%	D:45%
18	A:23%	B:18%	C:14%	D:45%	42	A:9%	B:27%	C:5%	D:59%
19	A:14%	B:50%	C:27%	D:9%	43	A:9%	B:82%	C:9%	D:0%
20	A:4%	B:55%	C:9%	D:32%	44	A:23%	B:9%	C:59%	D:9%
21	A:27%	B:27%	C:23%	D:23%	45	A:45%	B:23%	C:9%	D:23%
22	A:13%	B:64%	C:23%	D:0%	46	A:77%	B:5%	C:9%	D:9%
23	A:55%	B:14%	C:27%	D:4%	47	A:55%	B:41%	C:0%	D:4%
24	A:9%	B:45%	C:32%	D:14%	48	A:0%	B:4%	C:64%	D:32%

£125,000

	A	B	C	D		A	B	C	D
1	A:26%	B:18%	C:4%	D:52%	5	A:9%	B:41%	C:18%	D:32%
2	A:23%	B:9%	C:36%	D:32%	6	A:27%	B:23%	C:50%	D:0%
3	A:31%	B:16%	C:22%	D:31%	7	A:18%	B:0%	C:77%	D:5%
4	A:36%	B:5%	C:23%	D:36%	8	A:50%	B:9%	C:18%	D:23%

ASK THE AUDIENCE

9	A:41%	B:36%	C:9%	D:14%	27	A:18%	B:82%	C:0%	D:0%
10	A:41%	B:18%	C:36%	D:5%	28	A:50%	B:27%	C:9%	D:14%
11	A:14%	B:8%	C:55%	D:23%	29	A:18%	B:14%	C:36%	D:32%
12	A:36%	B:23%	C:32%	D:9%	30	A:32%	B:41%	C:18%	D:9%
13	A:14%	B:36%	C:36%	D:14%	31	A:36%	B:18%	C:23%	D:23%
14	A:36%	B:50%	C:14%	D:0%	32	A:82%	B:4%	C:0%	D:14%
15	A:23%	B:41%	C:27%	D:9%	33	A:9%	B:27%	C:55%	D:9%
16	A:32%	B:9%	C:32%	D:27%	34	A:36%	B:32%	C:27%	D:5%
17	A:32%	B:9%	C:14%	D:45%	35	A:32%	B:36%	C:23%	D:9%
18	A:18%	B:45%	C:27%	D:10%	36	A:50%	B:32%	C:9%	D:9%
19	A:32%	B:23%	C:41%	D:4%	37	A:18%	B:50%	C:5%	D:27%
20	A:45%	B:5%	C:50%	D:0%	38	A:18%	B:23%	C:50%	D:9%
21	A:32%	B:45%	C:5%	D:18%	39	A:32%	B:41%	C:18%	D:9%
22	A:45%	B:23%	C:9%	D:23%	40	A:5%	B:13%	C:77%	D:5%
23	A:18%	B:32%	C:18%	D:32%	41	A:55%	B:14%	C:8%	D:23%
24	A:32%	B:23%	C:32%	D:13%	42	A:23%	B:31%	C:23%	D:23%
25	A:36%	B:41%	C:9%	D:14%	43	A:27%	B:36%	C:32%	D:5%
26	A:14%	B:68%	C:14%	D:4%	44	A:18%	B:41%	C:23%	D:18%

£250,000

1	A:15%	B:30%	C:30%	D:25%	21	A:25%	B:5%	C:55%	D:15%
2	A:20%	B:55%	C:15%	D:10%	22	A:10%	B:25%	C:5%	D:60%
3	A:30%	B:25%	C:40%	D:5%	23	A:5%	B:25%	C:55%	D:15%
4	A:20%	B:30%	C:20%	D:30%	24	A:0%	B:15%	C:25%	D:60%
5	A:30%	B:30%	C:20%	D:20%	25	A:25%	B:45%	C:15%	D:15%
6	A:25%	B:20%	C:15%	D:40%	26	A:10%	B:75%	C:5%	D:10%
7	A:10%	B:40%	C:25%	D:25%	27	A:5%	B:20%	C:60%	D:15%
8	A:15%	B:30%	C:10%	D:45%	28	A:30%	B:35%	C:15%	D:20%
9	A:20%	B:30%	C:15%	D:35%	29	A:5%	B:25%	C:50%	D:20%
10	A:35%	B:25%	C:20%	D:20%	30	A:25%	B:15%	C:35%	D:25%
11	A:80%	B:5%	C:15%	D:0%	31	A:60%	B:20%	C:15%	D:5%
12	A:30%	B:20%	C:45%	D:5%	32	A:30%	B:65%	C:5%	D:0%
13	A:50%	B:10%	C:10%	D:30%	33	A:10%	B:10%	C:15%	D:65%
14	A:20%	B:50%	C:20%	D:10%	34	A:65%	B:10%	C:10%	D:15%
15	A:5%	B:40%	C:20%	D:35%	35	A:15%	B:45%	C:30%	D:10%
16	A:25%	B:30%	C:15%	D:30%	36	A:0%	B:35%	C:40%	D:25%
17	A:10%	B:10%	C:65%	D:15%	37	A:10%	B:85%	C:5%	D:0%
18	A:0%	B:15%	C:60%	D:25%	38	A:5%	B:20%	C:30%	D:45%
19	A:10%	B:70%	C:0%	D:20%	39	A:40%	B:25%	C:25%	D:10%
20	A:15%	B:30%	C:50%	D:5%	40	A:15%	B:60%	C:15%	D:10%

ASK THE AUDIENCE

£500,000

	A	B	C	D
1	15%	50%	10%	25%
2	10%	10%	15%	65%
3	45%	15%	10%	30%
4	40%	25%	20%	15%
5	25%	30%	30%	15%
6	15%	25%	5%	55%
7	5%	25%	30%	40%
8	35%	15%	5%	45%
9	10%	20%	60%	10%
10	30%	10%	50%	10%
11	5%	30%	65%	0%
12	40%	30%	20%	10%
13	35%	35%	15%	15%
14	0%	15%	45%	40%
15	5%	70%	0%	25%
16	15%	45%	40%	0%
17	5%	45%	30%	20%
18	10%	40%	40%	10%
19	35%	20%	45%	0%
20	10%	20%	25%	45%
21	10%	20%	25%	45%
22	20%	55%	5%	20%
23	35%	45%	15%	5%
24	10%	65%	10%	15%
25	10%	35%	25%	30%
26	15%	15%	35%	35%
27	20%	10%	10%	60%
28	50%	20%	20%	10%
29	5%	20%	35%	40%
30	50%	25%	15%	10%
31	25%	50%	10%	15%
32	25%	30%	30%	15%
33	30%	30%	35%	5%
34	0%	5%	5%	90%
35	60%	15%	10%	15%
36	20%	15%	15%	50%

£1,000,000

	A	B	C	D
1	5%	75%	5%	15%
2	10%	20%	55%	15%
3	50%	30%	15%	5%
4	20%	25%	5%	50%
5	0%	50%	10%	40%
6	5%	45%	35%	15%
7	35%	5%	10%	50%
8	10%	40%	25%	25%
9	25%	35%	10%	30%
10	30%	35%	20%	15%
11	10%	35%	20%	35%
12	15%	25%	10%	50%
13	45%	25%	25%	5%
14	20%	30%	30%	20%
15	55%	30%	5%	10%
16	75%	5%	5%	15%
17	25%	55%	10%	10%
18	65%	10%	15%	10%
19	15%	40%	25%	20%
20	15%	45%	30%	10%
21	20%	0%	25%	55%
22	10%	30%	50%	10%
23	50%	20%	20%	10%
24	70%	10%	15%	5%
25	45%	25%	15%	15%
26	15%	30%	45%	10%
27	5%	25%	20%	50%
28	60%	5%	15%	20%
29	25%	20%	50%	5%
30	15%	10%	65%	10%
31	35%	30%	25%	10%
32	15%	15%	5%	65%

Answers

Fastest Finger First

1	DBCA	2	DACB	3	CBAD	4	CDAB	5	CADB
6	DACB	7	CDAB	8	CABD	9	CABD	10	DBCA
11	DABC	12	BCDA	13	DCAB	14	BADC	15	BACD
16	CDAB	17	CBDA	18	ADCB	19	CDBA	20	CABD
21	BADC	22	CADB	23	CBAD	24	CADB	25	DCAB
26	BDAC	27	BADC	28	BDAC	29	BDAC	30	DACB
31	BADC	32	DBCA	33	CBDA	34	CADB	35	CBAD
36	DCAB	37	CDBA	38	DBCA	39	CADB	40	DCAB
41	CBAD	42	CADB	43	CBDA	44	BDCA	45	BDAC
46	DCBA	47	BDCA	48	DACB	49	CADB	50	CBDA
51	CBDA	52	CDBA	53	DACB	54	CBAD	55	BDCA
56	BCDA	57	DCAB	58	BADC	59	BDCA	60	ADBC
61	DBAC	62	CBAD	63	BDAC	64	BACD	65	BDCA
66	BDAC	67	DBAC	68	BCDA	69	CDAB	70	DBCA
71	DBCA	72	CBDA	73	BCAD	74	BDCA	75	BADC
76	BDCA	77	BDCA	78	CDBA	79	ACDB	80	BDAC
81	ACBD	82	DBCA	83	BCAD	84	BADC	85	BDCA
86	DBAC	87	BADC	88	CBDA	89	DBAC	90	DBAC
91	BDAC	92	CDBA	93	BADC	94	BDCA	95	BCDA
96	CADB	97	DBAC	98	CBAD	99	DBCA	100	BDCA

If you answered correctly, well done! Turn to page 31 to play for £100!

£100

1	B	2	D	3	C	4	B	5	A	6	D	7	D
8	A	9	A	10	B	11	B	12	C	13	D	14	B
15	A	16	D	17	C	18	B	19	B	20	B	21	D
22	B	23	A	24	A	25	D	26	D	27	B	28	A
29	C	30	A	31	B	32	C	33	D	34	A	35	B
36	C	37	D	38	A	39	C	40	A	41	C	42	B
43	C	44	D	45	B	46	B	47	D	48	C	49	D
50	D	51	B	52	C	53	C	54	C	55	D	56	A

ANSWERS

57 D	58 D	59 D	60 B	61 B	62 A	63 D
64 D	65 A	66 C	67 A	68 C	69 D	70 C
71 C	72 C	73 A	74 D	75 B	76 D	77 B
78 B	79 B	80 A	81 A	82 A	83 C	84 A
85 D	86 D	87 A	88 D			

If you have won £100, well done! Turn to page 51 to play for £200!

£200

1 C	2 B	3 B	4 A	5 C	6 D	7 B
8 B	9 D	10 C	11 B	12 B	13 A	14 D
15 B	16 B	17 D	18 B	19 A	20 D	21 C
22 A	23 B	24 B	25 D	26 B	27 D	28 R
29 D	30 B	31 D	32 C	33 C	34 A	35 B
36 B	37 D	38 C	39 A	40 C	41 A	42 B
43 D	44 D	45 B	46 B	47 D	48 C	49 D
50 B	51 C	52 D	53 B	54 A	55 B	56 B
57 C	58 B	59 A	60 C	61 D	62 D	63 D
64 D	65 C	66 A	67 A	68 B	69 D	70 B
71 B	72 B	73 B	74 B	75 B	76 C	77 B
78 B	79 B	80 D	81 C	82 A	83 C	84 C

If you have won £200, well done! Turn to page 69 to play for £300!

£300

1 C	2 A	3 D	4 C	5 D	6 A	7 A
8 A	9 B	10 A	11 D	12 A	13 C	14 A
15 B	16 C	17 B	18 B	19 B	20 A	21 C
22 A	23 D	24 D	25 C	26 A	27 B	28 C
29 B	30 A	31 D	32 A	33 B	34 C	35 D
36 B	37 A	38 B	39 B	40 C	41 B	42 A
43 A	44 C	45 B	46 C	47 B	48 B	49 A
50 B	51 C	52 B	53 A	54 D	55 C	56 C
57 B	58 D	59 A	60 A	61 B	62 D	63 D
64 B	65 D	66 D	67 B	68 A	69 D	70 A
71 B	72 B	73 B	74 D	75 B	76 D	77 C
78 B	79 B	80 A				

If you have won £300, well done! Turn to page 87 to play for £500!

ANSWERS

£500

1	A	2	B	3	A	4	C	5	A	6	B	7	D
8	B	9	C	10	C	11	B	12	B	13	B	14	A
15	C	16	D	17	A	18	A	19	B	20	B	21	D
22	D	23	B	24	B	25	C	26	D	27	A	28	A
29	A	30	C	31	A	32	A	33	C	34	C	35	D
36	B	37	A	38	A	39	B	40	D	41	B	42	C
43	C	44	D	45	A	46	B	47	B	48	A	49	D
50	D	51	C	52	C	53	B	54	A	55	C	56	B
57	D	58	C	59	D	60	D	61	C	62	D	63	C
64	C	65	B	66	C	67	B	68	B	69	C	70	A
71	C	72	D	73	A	74	A	75	D	76	B		

If you have won £500, well done! Turn to page 105 to play for £1,000!

£1,000

1	B	2	D	3	B	4	D	5	D	6	A	7	D
8	C	9	D	10	B	11	C	12	C	13	D	14	C
15	B	16	A	17	A	18	D	19	D	20	B	21	B
22	B	23	B	24	D	25	C	26	A	27	C	28	D
29	C	30	A	31	B	32	C	33	B	34	D	35	D
36	B	37	D	38	D	39	B	40	C	41	B	42	D
43	C	44	D	45	C	46	B	47	C	48	C	49	C
50	D	51	A	52	D	53	B	54	D	55	A	56	D
57	C	58	B	59	B	60	A	61	C	62	B	63	A
64	B	65	D	66	A	67	B	68	D	69	D	70	B
71	B	72	B										

If you have won £1,000, well done! Turn to page 121 to play for £2,000!

£2,000

1	B	2	D	3	C	4	D	5	D	6	B	7	C
8	A	9	C	10	D	11	C	12	A	13	B	14	A
15	C	16	A	17	B	18	B	19	D	20	A	21	A
22	D	23	C	24	B	25	C	26	B	27	D	28	D
29	C	30	A	31	C	32	A	33	D	34	A	35	A
36	B	37	C	38	D	39	A	40	D	41	A	42	D
43	D	44	B	45	A	46	C	47	D	48	D	49	D
50	B	51	C	52	B	53	A	54	C	55	A	56	C
57	C	58	C	59	D	60	D	61	B	62	D	63	B
64	C	65	D	66	D	67	D	68	D				

If you have won £2,000, well done! Turn to page 137 to play for £4,000!

ANSWERS

£4,000

1 B	2 C	3 B	4 B	5 A	6 B	7 D
8 B	9 D	10 C	11 C	12 C	13 B	14 D
15 A	16 A	17 B	18 B	19 B	20 B	21 C
22 C	23 A	24 B	25 C	26 B	27 D	28 C
29 C	30 A	31 A	32 A	33 A	34 B	35 B
36 D	37 A	38 C	39 B	40 C	41 B	42 D
43 B	44 B	45 A	46 C	47 A	48 C	49 D
50 B	51 B	52 C	53 D	54 C	55 D	56 D
57 A	58 B	59 C	60 B	61 C	62 D	63 C
64 B						

If you have won £4,000, well done! Turn to page 151 to play for £8,000!

£8,000

1 C	2 B	3 B	4 D	5 B	6 D	7 A
8 B	9 B	10 B	11 A	12 D	13 D	14 D
15 B	16 B	17 C	18 C	19 A	20 D	21 A
22 A	23 A	24 A	25 A	26 B	27 C	28 C
29 C	30 D	31 D	32 B	33 D	34 B	35 A
36 B	37 D	38 C	39 C	40 A	41 D	42 D
43 C	44 D	45 A	46 A	47 A	48 B	49 D
50 B	51 A	52 A	53 B	54 B	55 D	56 B
57 D	58 D	59 D	60 B			

If you have won £8,000, well done! Turn to page 165 to play for £16,000!

£16,000

1 D	2 C	3 C	4 A	5 C	6 C	7 C
8 A	9 C	10 B	11 B	12 D	13 D	14 C
15 B	16 B	17 B	18 B	19 C	20 B	21 C
22 A	23 D	24 B	25 B	26 C	27 A	28 D
29 A	30 C	31 D	32 C	33 C	34 B	35 A
36 B	37 D	38 A	39 D	40 C	41 A	42 D
43 B	44 C	45 C	46 D	47 B	48 B	49 C
50 A	51 A	52 B	53 C	54 C	55 B	56 C

If you have won £16,000, well done! Turn to page 179 to play for £32,000!

ANSWERS

£32,000

1	B	2	B	3	B	4	D	5	A	6	D	7	C
8	C	9	C	10	B	11	A	12	A	13	C	14	C
15	C	16	A	17	B	18	B	19	C	20	C	21	D
22	C	23	C	24	C	25	B	26	B	27	D	28	D
29	B	30	C	31	D	32	A	33	B	34	B	35	B
36	D	37	A	38	B	39	C	40	D	41	D	42	B
43	B	44	C	45	B	46	B	47	D	48	C	49	C
50	C	51	D	52	B								

If you have won £32,000, well done! Turn to page 191 to play for £64,000!

£64,000

1	B	2	D	3	B	4	D	5	A	6	C	7	D
8	C	9	C	10	C	11	B	12	D	13	C	14	D
15	D	16	A	17	D	18	D	19	B	20	D	21	B
22	B	23	C	24	B	25	C	26	C	27	A	28	D
29	B	30	D	31	B	32	C	33	D	34	C	35	B
36	A	37	C	38	D	39	C	40	A	41	D	42	D
43	B	44	C	45	D	46	A	47	B	48	C		

If you have won £64,000, well done! Turn to page 203 to play for £125,000!

£125,000

1	A	2	D	3	C	4	A	5	B	6	C	7	C
8	D	9	A	10	A	11	C	12	B	13	C	14	B
15	D	16	A	17	D	18	B	19	B	20	C	21	B
22	D	23	D	24	A	25	D	26	B	27	B	28	B
29	D	30	C	31	A	32	B	33	C	34	C	35	A
36	B	37	D	38	B	39	B	40	C	41	A	42	C
43	B	44	C										

If you have won £125,000, well done! Turn to page 213 to play for £250,000!

£250,000

1	A	2	B	3	A	4	C	5	C	6	A	7	B
8	D	9	D	10	B	11	A	12	B	13	D	14	B
15	B	16	B	17	C	18	D	19	C	20	A	21	C
22	D	23	B	24	C	25	B	26	B	27	C	28	D
29	D	30	A	31	B	32	A	33	D	34	A	35	C
36	D	37	A	38	B	39	D	40	C				

If you have won £250,000, well done! Turn to page 223 to play for £500,000!

ANSWERS

£500,000

1	C	2	C	3	A	4	B	5	C	6	A	7 C
8	B	9	C	10	A	11	C	12	C	13	B	14 C
15	C	16	C	17	A	18	A	19	B	20	C	21 D
22	A	23	B	24	D	25	A	26	D	27	D	28 A
29	C	30	A	31	B	32	B	33	C	34	D	35 B
36	B											

If you have won £500,000, well done! Turn to page 233 to play for £1,000,000!

£1,000,000

1	B	2	C	3	B	4	A	5	D	6	C	7 D
8	D	9	B	10	B	11	C	12	B	13	A	14 B
15	A	16	D	17	B	18	C	19	D	20	B	21 D
22	B	23	B	24	C	25	C	26	A	27	C	28 C
29	C	30	C	31	D	32	B						

If you have won £1,000,000, well done! You're a millionaire!

Score sheets

Write your name and the names of any other contestants in the space provided. Shade in each of the boxes lightly with a pencil once you or one of your fellow contestants has won the amount in that box. If you or any of the other contestants answer a question incorrectly and are out of the game, use a soft eraser to rub out the relevant boxes so that the final score is showing.

SCORE SHEET

contestant's name

....

50:50

15	£1 MILLION
14	£500,000
13	£250,000
12	£125,000
11	£64,000
10	£32,000
9	£16,000
8	£8,000
7	£4,000
6	£2,000
5	£1,000
4	£500
3	£300
2	£200
1	£100

contestant's name

....

50:50

15	£1 MILLION
14	£500,000
13	£250,000
12	£125,000
11	£64,000
10	£32,000
9	£16,000
8	£8,000
7	£4,000
6	£2,000
5	£1,000
4	£500
3	£300
2	£200
1	£100

SCORE SHEET

contestant's name		contestant's name	
....		....	

50:50	☎	👥	50:50	☎	👥
☐	☐	☐	☐	☐	☐

15	£1 MILLION	15	£1 MILLION
14	£500,000	14	£500,000
13	£250,000	13	£250,000
12	£125,000	12	£125,000
11	£64,000	11	£64,000
10	£32,000	10	£32,000
9	£16,000	9	£16,000
8	£8,000	8	£8,000
7	£4,000	7	£4,000
6	£2,000	6	£2,000
5	£1,000	5	£1,000
4	£500	4	£500
3	£300	3	£300
2	£200	2	£200
1	£100	1	£100

SCORE SHEET

contestant's name	contestant's name
....	....

50:50	☎	👥		50:50	☎	👥
☐	☐	☐		☐	☐	☐

15	£1 MILLION		15	£1 MILLION
14	£500,000		14	£500,000
13	£250,000		13	£250,000
12	£125,000		12	£125,000
11	£64,000		11	£64,000
10	£32,000		10	£32,000
9	£16,000		9	£16,000
8	£8,000		8	£8,000
7	£4,000		7	£4,000
6	£2,000		6	£2,000
5	£1,000		5	£1,000
4	£500		4	£500
3	£300		3	£300
2	£200		2	£200
1	£100		1	£100

SCORE SHEET

contestant's name	contestant's name
....	....
50:50 📞 👥	50:50 📞 👥
☐ ☐ ☐	☐ ☐ ☐

15	£1 MILLION	15	£1 MILLION
14	£500,000	14	£500,000
13	£250,000	13	£250,000
12	£125,000	12	£125,000
11	£64,000	11	£64,000
10	£32,000	10	£32,000
9	£16,000	9	£16,000
8	£8,000	8	£8,000
7	£4,000	7	£4,000
6	£2,000	6	£2,000
5	£1,000	5	£1,000
4	£500	4	£500
3	£300	3	£300
2	£200	2	£200
1	£100	1	£100

SCORE SHEET

contestant's name	contestant's name
....	....

50:50 📞 👥👥👥   50:50 📞 👥👥👥

☐ ☐ ☐   ☐ ☐ ☐

15	£1 MILLION	15	£1 MILLION
14	£500,000	14	£500,000
13	£250,000	13	£250,000
12	£125,000	12	£125,000
11	£64,000	11	£64,000
10	£32,000	10	£32,000
9	£16,000	9	£16,000
8	£8,000	8	£8,000
7	£4,000	7	£4,000
6	£2,000	6	£2,000
5	£1,000	5	£1,000
4	£500	4	£500
3	£300	3	£300
2	£200	2	£200
1	£100	1	£100

SCORE SHEET

contestant's name	contestant's name
....	....

50:50			50:50		
☐	☐	☐	☐	☐	☐

15	£1 MILLION		15	£1 MILLION
14	£500,000		14	£500,000
13	£250,000		13	£250,000
12	£125,000		12	£125,000
11	£64,000		11	£64,000
10	£32,000		10	£32,000
9	£16,000		9	£16,000
8	£8,000		8	£8,000
7	£4,000		7	£4,000
6	£2,000		6	£2,000
5	£1,000		5	£1,000
4	£500		4	£500
3	£300		3	£300
2	£200		2	£200
1	£100		1	£100

SCORE SHEET

contestant's name	contestant's name
....	....

50:50			50:50		
☐	☐	☐	☐	☐	☐

15	£1 MILLION		**15**	£1 MILLION
14	£500,000		**14**	£500,000
13	£250,000		**13**	£250,000
12	£125,000		**12**	£125,000
11	£64,000		**11**	£64,000
10	£32,000		**10**	£32,000
9	£16,000		**9**	£16,000
8	£8,000		**8**	£8,000
7	£4,000		**7**	£4,000
6	£2,000		**6**	£2,000
5	£1,000		**5**	£1,000
4	£500		**4**	£500
3	£300		**3**	£300
2	£200		**2**	£200
1	£100		**1**	£100

SCORE SHEET

contestant's name	contestant's name
....	....

50:50 · phone · audience

☐ ☐ ☐   ☐ ☐ ☐

15	£1 MILLION	15	£1 MILLION
14	£500,000	14	£500,000
13	£250,000	13	£250,000
12	£125,000	12	£125,000
11	£64,000	11	£64,000
10	£32,000	**10**	£32,000
9	£16,000	9	£16,000
8	£8,000	8	£8,000
7	£4,000	7	£4,000
6	£2,000	6	£2,000
5	£1,000	**5**	£1,000
4	£500	4	£500
3	£300	3	£300
2	£200	2	£200
1	£100	1	£100

SCORE SHEET

contestant's name

....

50:50

contestant's name

....

50:50

15	£1 MILLION	15	£1 MILLION
14	£500,000	14	£500,000
13	£250,000	13	£250,000
12	£125,000	12	£125,000
11	£64,000	11	£64,000
10	£32,000	10	£32,000
9	£16,000	9	£16,000
8	£8,000	8	£8,000
7	£4,000	7	£4,000
6	£2,000	6	£2,000
5	£1,000	5	£1,000
4	£500	4	£500
3	£300	3	£300
2	£200	2	£200
1	£100	1	£100

SCORE SHEET

contestant's name

....

50:50 ☎ 👥

☐ ☐ ☐

15	£1 MILLION
14	£500,000
13	£250,000
12	£125,000
11	£64,000
10	£32,000
9	£16,000
8	£8,000
7	£4,000
6	£2,000
5	£1,000
4	£500
3	£300
2	£200
1	£100

contestant's name

....

50:50 ☎ 👥

☐ ☐ ☐

15	£1 MILLION
14	£500,000
13	£250,000
12	£125,000
11	£64,000
10	£32,000
9	£16,000
8	£8,000
7	£4,000
6	£2,000
5	£1,000
4	£500
3	£300
2	£200
1	£100

SCORE SHEET

contestant's name

....

50:50 ⚡☎ 👥👥👥

☐ ☐ ☐

15	£1 MILLION
14	£500,000
13	£250,000
12	£125,000
11	£64,000
10	£32,000
9	£16,000
8	£8,000
7	£4,000
6	£2,000
5	£1,000
4	£500
3	£300
2	£200
1	£100

contestant's name

....

50:50 ⚡☎ 👥👥👥

☐ ☐ ☐

15	£1 MILLION
14	£500,000
13	£250,000
12	£125,000
11	£64,000
10	£32,000
9	£16,000
8	£8,000
7	£4,000
6	£2,000
5	£1,000
4	£500
3	£300
2	£200
1	£100

SCORE SHEET

contestant's name	contestant's name
....	....
50:50 ☎ 👥	50:50 ☎ 👥
☐ ☐ ☐	☐ ☐ ☐

15	£1 MILLION	15	£1 MILLION
14	£500,000	14	£500,000
13	£250,000	13	£250,000
12	£125,000	12	£125,000
11	£64,000	11	£64,000
10	£32,000	10	£32,000
9	£16,000	9	£16,000
8	£8,000	8	£8,000
7	£4,000	7	£4,000
6	£2,000	6	£2,000
5	£1,000	5	£1,000
4	£500	4	£500
3	£300	3	£300
2	£200	2	£200
1	£100	1	£100

SCORE SHEET

contestant's name

....

50:50 ☎ 👥
☐ ☐ ☐

15	£1 MILLION
14	£500,000
13	£250,000
12	£125,000
11	£64,000
10	£32,000
9	£16,000
8	£8,000
7	£4,000
6	£2,000
5	£1,000
4	£500
3	£300
2	£200
1	£100

contestant's name

....

50:50 ☎ 👥
☐ ☐ ☐

15	£1 MILLION
14	£500,000
13	£250,000
12	£125,000
11	£64,000
10	£32,000
9	£16,000
8	£8,000
7	£4,000
6	£2,000
5	£1,000
4	£500
3	£300
2	£200
1	£100

S C O R E   S H E E T

contestant's name	contestant's name
....	....

15	£1 MILLION	15	£1 MILLION
14	£500,000	14	£500,000
13	£250,000	13	£250,000
12	£125,000	12	£125,000
11	£64,000	11	£64,000
10	£32,000	10	£32,000
9	£16,000	9	£16,000
8	£8,000	8	£8,000
7	£4,000	7	£4,000
6	£2,000	6	£2,000
5	£1,000	5	£1,000
4	£500	4	£500
3	£300	3	£300
2	£200	2	£200
1	£100	1	£100

SCORE SHEET

contestant's name	contestant's name
....	....

50:50			50:50		
☐	☐	☐	☐	☐	☐

15	£1 MILLION	15	£1 MILLION
14	£500,000	14	£500,000
13	£250,000	13	£250,000
12	£125,000	12	£125,000
11	£64,000	11	£64,000
10	£32,000	10	£32,000
9	£16,000	9	£16,000
8	£8,000	8	£8,000
7	£4,000	7	£4,000
6	£2,000	6	£2,000
5	£1,000	5	£1,000
4	£500	4	£500
3	£300	3	£300
2	£200	2	£200
1	£100	1	£100

SCORE SHEET

contestant's name		contestant's name	

50:50	✂	👥	50:50	✂	👥
☐	☐	☐	☐	☐	☐

15	£1 MILLION	15	£1 MILLION
14	£500,000	14	£500,000
13	£250,000	13	£250,000
12	£125,000	12	£125,000
11	£64,000	11	£64,000
10	£32,000	**10**	£32,000
9	£16,000	9	£16,000
8	£8,000	8	£8,000
7	£4,000	7	£4,000
6	£2,000	6	£2,000
5	£1,000	**5**	£1,000
4	£500	4	£500
3	£300	3	£300
2	£200	2	£200
1	£100	1	£100

SCORE SHEET

15	£1 MILLION
14	£500,000
13	£250,000
12	£125,000
11	£64,000
10	£32,000
9	£16,000
8	£8,000
7	£4,000
6	£2,000
5	£1,000
4	£500
3	£300
2	£200
1	£100

contestant's name

....

50:50 📞 👥 👥 👥

☐ ☐ ☐

15	£1 MILLION
14	£500,000
13	£250,000
12	£125,000
11	£64,000
10	£32,000
9	£16,000
8	£8,000
7	£4,000
6	£2,000
5	£1,000
4	£500
3	£300
2	£200
1	£100

SCORE SHEET

contestant's name	contestant's name
....	....

50:50	☎	👥		50:50	☎	👥
☐	☐	☐		☐	☐	☐

15	£1 MILLION		15	£1 MILLION
14	£500,000		14	£500,000
13	£250,000		13	£250,000
12	£125,000		12	£125,000
11	£64,000		11	£64,000
10	£32,000		10	£32,000
9	£16,000		9	£16,000
8	£8,000		8	£8,000
7	£4,000		7	£4,000
6	£2,000		6	£2,000
5	£1,000		5	£1,000
4	£500		4	£500
3	£300		3	£300
2	£200		2	£200
1	£100		1	£100

SCORE SHEET

50:50	☎	👥
☐	☐	☐

50:50	☎	👥
☐	☐	☐

15	£1 MILLION
14	£500,000
13	£250,000
12	£125,000
11	£64,000
10	£32,000
9	£16,000
8	£8,000
7	£4,000
6	£2,000
5	£1,000
4	£500
3	£300
2	£200
1	£100

15	£1 MILLION
14	£500,000
13	£250,000
12	£125,000
11	£64,000
10	£32,000
9	£16,000
8	£8,000
7	£4,000
6	£2,000
5	£1,000
4	£500
3	£300
2	£200
1	£100

SCORE SHEET

contestant's name		contestant's name	
....		....	

50:50	☎	👥	50:50	☎	👥
☐	☐	☐	☐	☐	☐

15	£1 MILLION	15	£1 MILLION
14	£500,000	14	£500,000
13	£250,000	13	£250,000
12	£125,000	12	£125,000
11	£64,000	11	£64,000
10	£32,000	10	£32,000
9	£16,000	9	£16,000
8	£8,000	8	£8,000
7	£4,000	7	£4,000
6	£2,000	6	£2,000
5	£1,000	5	£1,000
4	£500	4	£500
3	£300	3	£300
2	£200	2	£200
1	£100	1	£100

SCORE SHEET

contestant's name

....

50:50   📞   👥👥

☐   ☐   ☐

15	£1 MILLION
14	£500,000
13	£250,000
12	£125,000
11	£64,000
10	£32,000
9	£16,000
8	£8,000
7	£4,000
6	£2,000
5	£1,000
4	£500
3	£300
2	£200
1	£100

contestant's name

....

50:50   📞   👥👥

☐   ☐   ☐

15	£1 MILLION
14	£500,000
13	£250,000
12	£125,000
11	£64,000
10	£32,000
9	£16,000
8	£8,000
7	£4,000
6	£2,000
5	£1,000
4	£500
3	£300
2	£200
1	£100

SCORE SHEET

contestant's name	contestant's name
....	....

50:50	📞	👥		50:50	📞	👥
☐	☐	☐		☐	☐	☐

15	£1 MILLION		15	£1 MILLION
14	£500,000		14	£500,000
13	£250,000		13	£250,000
12	£125,000		12	£125,000
11	£64,000		11	£64,000
10	£32,000		10	£32,000
9	£16,000		9	£16,000
8	£8,000		8	£8,000
7	£4,000		7	£4,000
6	£2,000		6	£2,000
5	£1,000		5	£1,000
4	£500		4	£500
3	£300		3	£300
2	£200		2	£200
1	£100		1	£100

SCORE SHEET

contestant's name		contestant's name	
....		....	

50:50	☎	👥		50:50	☎	👥
☐	☐	☐		☐	☐	☐

15	£1 MILLION	15	£1 MILLION
14	£500,000	14	£500,000
13	£250,000	13	£250,000
12	£125,000	12	£125,000
11	£64,000	11	£64,000
10	£32,000	10	£32,000
9	£16,000	9	£16,000
8	£8,000	8	£8,000
7	£4,000	7	£4,000
6	£2,000	6	£2,000
5	£1,000	5	£1,000
4	£500	4	£500
3	£300	3	£300
2	£200	2	£200
1	£100	1	£100

SCORE SHEET

contestant's name	contestant's name
....	....

50:50 · · · □ □ □   50:50 · · · □ □ □

15	£1 MILLION	15	£1 MILLION
14	£500,000	14	£500,000
13	£250,000	13	£250,000
12	£125,000	12	£125,000
11	£64,000	11	£64,000
10	£32,000	10	£32,000
9	£16,000	9	£16,000
8	£8,000	8	£8,000
7	£4,000	7	£4,000
6	£2,000	6	£2,000
5	£1,000	5	£1,000
4	£500	4	£500
3	£300	3	£300
2	£200	2	£200
1	£100	1	£100

S C O R E   S H E E T

....

....

50:50

15	£1 MILLION
14	£500,000
13	£250,000
12	£125,000
11	£64,000
10	£32,000
9	£16,000
8	£8,000
7	£4,000
6	£2,000
5	£1,000
4	£500
3	£300
2	£200
1	£100

15	£1 MILLION
14	£500,000
13	£250,000
12	£125,000
11	£64,000
10	£32,000
9	£16,000
8	£8,000
7	£4,000
6	£2,000
5	£1,000
4	£500
3	£300
2	£200
1	£100

SCORE SHEET

contestant's name		contestant's name	
....		....	

| 50:50 ⚡☎ 👥👥👥 | | 50:50 ⚡☎ 👥👥👥 | |
| ☐ ☐ ☐ | | ☐ ☐ ☐ | |

15	£1 MILLION	15	£1 MILLION
14	£500,000	14	£500,000
13	£250,000	13	£250,000
12	£125,000	12	£125,000
11	£64,000	11	£64,000
10	£32,000	10	£32,000
9	£16,000	9	£16,000
8	£8,000	8	£8,000
7	£4,000	7	£4,000
6	£2,000	6	£2,000
5	£1,000	5	£1,000
4	£500	4	£500
3	£300	3	£300
2	£200	2	£200
1	£100	1	£100

SCORE SHEET

contestant's name	contestant's name
....	....

50:50			50:50		
☐	☐	☐	☐	☐	☐

15	£1 MILLION	15	£1 MILLION
14	£500,000	14	£500,000
13	£250,000	13	£250,000
12	£125,000	12	£125,000
11	£64,000	11	£64,000
10	£32,000	10	£32,000
9	£16,000	9	£16,000
8	£8,000	8	£8,000
7	£4,000	7	£4,000
6	£2,000	6	£2,000
5	£1,000	5	£1,000
4	£500	4	£500
3	£300	3	£300
2	£200	2	£200
1	£100	1	£100

SCORE SHEET

contestant's name	contestant's name
....	....

50:50 📞 👥	50:50 📞 👥
☐ ☐ ☐	☐ ☐ ☐

15	£1 MILLION	15	£1 MILLION
14	£500,000	14	£500,000
13	£250,000	13	£250,000
12	£125,000	12	£125,000
11	£64,000	11	£64,000
10	£32,000	10	£32,000
9	£16,000	9	£16,000
8	£8,000	8	£8,000
7	£4,000	7	£4,000
6	£2,000	6	£2,000
5	£1,000	5	£1,000
4	£500	4	£500
3	£300	3	£300
2	£200	2	£200
1	£100	1	£100

SCORE SHEET

contestant's name		
....		
50:50	⚡📞	👥👥
☐	☐	☐

15	£1 MILLION	15	£1 MILLION
14	£500,000	14	£500,000
13	£250,000	13	£250,000
12	£125,000	12	£125,000
11	£64,000	11	£64,000
10	£32,000	**10**	£32,000
9	£16,000	9	£16,000
8	£8,000	8	£8,000
7	£4,000	7	£4,000
6	£2,000	6	£2,000
5	£1,000	**5**	£1,000
4	£500	4	£500
3	£300	3	£300
2	£200	2	£200
1	£100	1	£100

SCORE SHEET

contestant's name	contestant's name
....	....

50:50	☎	👥👥		50:50	☎	👥👥
☐	☐	☐		☐	☐	☐

15	£1 MILLION		15	£1 MILLION
14	£500,000		14	£500,000
13	£250,000		13	£250,000
12	£125,000		12	£125,000
11	£64,000		11	£64,000
10	£32,000		10	£32,000
9	£16,000		9	£16,000
8	£8,000		8	£8,000
7	£4,000		7	£4,000
6	£2,000		6	£2,000
5	£1,000		5	£1,000
4	£500		4	£500
3	£300		3	£300
2	£200		2	£200
1	£100		1	£100

SCORE SHEET

15	£1 MILLION
14	£500,000
13	£250,000
12	£125,000
11	£64,000
10	£32,000
9	£16,000
8	£8,000
7	£4,000
6	£2,000
5	£1,000
4	£500
3	£300
2	£200
1	£100

15	£1 MILLION
14	£500,000
13	£250,000
12	£125,000
11	£64,000
10	£32,000
9	£16,000
8	£8,000
7	£4,000
6	£2,000
5	£1,000
4	£500
3	£300
2	£200
1	£100